Natural Language
Data Management and Interfaces

Synthesis Lectures on Data Management

Editor
H.V. Jagadish, *University of Michigan*

Founding Editor
M. Tamer Özsu, *University of Waterloo*

Synthesis Lectures on Data Management is edited by H.V. Jagadish of the University of Michigan. The series publishes 80–150 page publications on topics pertaining to data management. Topics include query languages, database system architectures, transaction management, data warehousing, XML and databases, data stream systems, wide scale data distribution, multimedia data management, data mining, and related subjects.

Natural Language Data Management and Interfaces

Yunyao Li and Davood Rafiei

ISBN: 978-3-031-00734-7   paperback
ISBN: 978-3-031-01862-6   ebook
ISBN: 978-3-031-00089-8   hardcover

DOI 10.1007/978-3-031-01862-6

A Publication in the Springer series
SYNTHESIS LECTURES ON DATA MANAGEMENT

Lecture #49
Series Editor: H.V. Jagadish, *University of Michigan*
Founding Editor: M. Tamer Özsu, *University of Waterloo*
Series ISSN
Print 2153-5418   Electronic 2153-5426

Natural Language
Data Management and Interfaces

Yunyao Li
IBM Research – Almaden

Davood Rafiei
University of Alberta

SYNTHESIS LECTURES ON DATA MANAGEMENT #49

ABSTRACT

The volume of natural language text data has been rapidly increasing over the past two decades, due to factors such as the growth of the Web, the low cost associated with publishing, and the progress on the digitization of printed texts. This growth combined with the proliferation of natural language systems for search and retrieving information provides tremendous opportunities for studying some of the areas where database systems and natural language processing systems overlap.

This book explores two interrelated and important areas of overlap: (1) managing natural language data and (2) developing natural language interfaces to databases. It presents relevant concepts and research questions, state-of-the-art methods, related systems, and research opportunities and challenges covering both areas. Relevant topics discussed on natural language data management include data models, data sources, queries, storage and indexing, and transforming natural language text. Under natural language interfaces, it presents the anatomy of these interfaces to databases, the challenges related to query understanding and query translation, and relevant aspects of user interactions. Each of the challenges is covered in a systematic way: first starting with a quick overview of the topics, followed by a comprehensive view of recent techniques that have been proposed to address the challenge along with illustrative examples. It also reviews some notable systems in details in terms of how they address different challenges and their contributions. Finally, it discusses open challenges and opportunities for natural language management and interfaces.

The goal of this book is to provide an introduction to the methods, problems, and solutions that are used in managing natural language data and building natural language interfaces to databases. It serves as a starting point for readers who are interested in pursuing additional work on these exciting topics in both academic and industrial environments.

KEYWORDS

natural language data, natural language interfaces, natural language queries, querying natural language text, semantic parsing, human computer interaction, conversational natural language interfaces

To my husband, Huahai,
  my son, Boyan,
  and my parents with love

                                                        Yunyao Li

To my wife, Malan,
  my children, Amin, Yasmin, and Ali,
  and my parents with love

                                                        Davood Rafiei

Contents

Preface

Natural languages are languages developed naturally by human through use and repetition. They are central to almost all human activities. In today's digital world, a large portion of data that is stored and exchanged is in natural languages. These languages also play a growing role in our daily interactions with machines with the popularization of voice-based interfaces such as self-driven cars and virtual personal assistants. Allowing "casual users" to employ their native languages today has implications for both communicating with databases and storing and retrieving data in the form of natural languages.

This book grew out of our passion for the two interrelated topics in the intersection of database systems and natural language processing: managing natural languages and building natural language interfaces to databases. Despite the commonality of the issues in understanding natural languages and dealing with ambiguities, each area offers some challenges of its own. In the former, the structure of the data is described informally in a natural language but the queries are more formal. In the latter, data is described more formally (e.g., in a relational database) but the queries are informally expressed in a natural language.

This goal of this book is to provide a unified view of both topics, with overlapping areas discussed once and/or cross-referenced. This book takes a structured approach to present a comprehensive survey of all important research problems and their key sub-problems and the latest development in the related fields. It also bridges the gap between everything-is-a-relation and everything-is-a-text cultures, highlighting where each culture shines and how it contributes to an integrated solution.

This book is suitable for database students, researchers, and developers who are interested in different aspects of managing natural language data and developing natural language interfaces to databases. It will also provide students, researchers, and practitioners in other related areas (such as natural language processing, question answering, information retrieval, data mining, and machine learning) with database principles and techniques that may be applicable to related problems in those areas.

The book may be used within various courses at graduate and undergraduate levels, as a starting point to the literature. A course covering natural language interfaces to databases may discuss Sections 4.1–4.4 for the main components, their functions and challenges, and one or more of the systems in Section 4.5, as relevant, for more details. A course covering querying and indexing natural language text may discuss Sections 3.3–3.5 and maybe Section 3.6. In both cases, any other section may be covered as relevant or applicable. Section 3.6 may also be covered within a course on linked data and semantic search. The background section may be skipped for those familiar with common natural language processing techniques. The book grew out of a three-hour tutorial on the same subject [Li and Rafiei, 2017], given by the authors at SIGMOD 2017. The slides used in the tutorial are available online and can be easily incorporated into courses.[1]

Yunyao Li and Davood Rafiei
July 2018

---

[1]https://webdocs.cs.ualberta.ca/~drafiei/papers/SIGMOD2017tutorial_LR.pdf and https://www.slides hare.net/YunyaoLi/natural-language-data-management-and-interfaces-recent-development-and-open-challenges

Acknowledgments

This book is made possible with the help and support of a number of people. H.V. Jagadish invited us to write this book after our SIGMOD 2017 tutorial, and Diane Cerra pushed us to stay within our timeline. We wish to thank both for their help and support. Joint work and discussions with our students and colleagues over the years helped shape the book. In particular, Davood wishes to thank Pirooz Chubak, Haobin Li, Dekang Lin, and Ehsan Kamalloo, and Yunyao wishes to thank Alan Akbik, Chris Baik, Ishan Chaudhuri, Laura Chiticariu, Ronald Fagin, Laura Haas, H.V. Jagadish, Benny Kimelfeld, Rajasekar Krishnamurthy, Sriram Raghavan, Lucian Popa, Frederick Reiss, Satinder P. Singh, Shivakumar Vaithyanathan, Huahai Yang, and Huaiyu Zhu. We are also grateful to our reviewers (Daniel Deutch, Sourav Bhowmick, and Laszlo Kovacs) who, despite their busy schedules, carefully read the initial draft of this book and provided detailed and constructive comments. We have taken each and every one of them into consideration while improving the book. Finally, we also wish to acknowledge our funding sources. Davood Rafiei's research is supported by the Natural Sciences and Engineering Research Council of Canada, and Yunyao Li's research is supported by IBM Research.

Yunyao Li and Davood Rafiei
July 2018

CHAPTER 1

Introduction

> If we are to satisfy the needs of casual users of data bases, we must break through
> the barriers that presently prevent these users from freely employing their native
> languages. — Ted Codd

Codd [1974] said the above quote in the context of Rendezvous, a dialog-based system he envisioned back in 1974 to allow casual users to effectively communicate with structured databases. At the time, structured data was the only source of data stored in machines due to limitations in machine resources and costs. Today a large portion of data stored and exchanged is in natural languages. These languages also play a much bigger role in our daily interactions with machines. Allowing "casual users" to employ their native languages today has implications for both communicating with databases and storing and retrieving data in the form of natural languages.

Extracting structured data from natural languages is typically done by information extraction systems. These systems can be classified into machine learning-based and rule-based. Machine learning-based methods require a significant amount of training data to train a model for a specific extraction task (e.g., companies and their headquarters). Rule-based systems take a more declarative approach for describing patterns or queries that extract the desired information. Even though machine learning-based methods may achieve a better accuracy when enough training data is provided, rule-based systems can be applied more broadly, since they do not need training data, and seem to be a more popular choice in industry as observed by Chiticariu et al. [2013] and Suganthan et al. [2015]. Also, the clarity of rule-based systems in explaining the information needs allows further analysis and integration with other data sources. This book covers more declarative approaches for querying and extracting information from natural language sources.

Databases are often considered as the cornerstone of modern society. Data residing in databases is essential to almost every aspect of our daily life (from electric patient record since birth to retirement account) as well as the business world (from accounting reports to invoicing customers). Structured queries in a formal database query language such as SQL help access data in databases in a meaningful and powerful way. However, in order to specify such queries, one needs to have either the knowledge of both the query language and underlying database schema or the availability of a pre-built search interface, usually supporting only limited types of search queries. Supporting querying databases in natural languages would enable users to naturally interact with databases without aforementioned limitations, and has long been regarded as the holy grail of database query interface.

Managing natural language data and building natural language interfaces to databases focus on complimentary aspects of data management. The former focuses on taming information from natural language to help populating data into databases, while the latter aims to drastically improve the accessibility of data already residing in databases. However, the two topics are highly interrelated to each other. Obviously, both deal with natural language. As a result, techniques for extracting information from natural language into structured data are also often applicable to building natural language interfaces to databases, and vise verse. We provide an overview for such techniques applicable to both (e.g., *semantic parsing*) in Chapter 2. Furthermore, managing natural language data brings additional challenges to building natural language interfaces to databases with new types of data and queries to support, while natural language interfaces to databases can potentially provide seamless integration of databases populated from heterogeneous data sources, including those in natural languages, with complete transparency to their users.

There have been two major developments that have made the two interrelated topics of managing natural language data and developing natural language interfaces to databases relevant and timely. First, we have a much larger set of resources at our disposal, in terms of the processing power, both public and proprietary data (e.g., Wikipedia, Twitter), and knowledge bases such as Yago [Suchanek et al., 2007], to build and develop techniques to better manage natural language data; furthermore, there is a growing number of tools that can help with processing text, ranging from part-of-speech taggers, to syntactic parsers, to semantic role labelers, to deep learning libraries. Second, the success of IBM's Watson [Ferrucci, 2012] at Jeopardy and the emergence of natural language dialog systems such as Apple's Siri, Google's Home, Amazon's Alexa, and Microsoft's Cortana has further ignited the interest in natural language data analysis and interfaces. These developments have two implications as far as database research is concerned. First, we are amassing natural language text in sizes that we have not seen before and the sheer volume of information encoded in text and its relationships to data in our relational databases is too great to be ignored. Second, there is a huge opportunity and demand to push database systems more in the direction of realizing Codd's vision of "rendezvous."

Numerous science fiction books and movies contain artificial intelligent characters who obtain their knowledge from a vast amount of data sources, including those in natural languages (e.g., books and scientific publications), and interact with human in natural languages. Obviously, the reality of today's technology is far from being able to enable artificial intelligent characters depicted in science fictions such as Data from *Star Trek* and Samantha from *Her*. Nonetheless, progress in managing natural language data and developing natural language interfaces to databases such as IBM's Watson and more recently Project Debater has already shown great promise in automatically harvesting information from massive natural language sources and leveraging such information to enable new generations of artificial intelligent systems and applications.

In this book, we explore these two fascinating topics. We review the state-of-the-art methods, recent progress, research opportunities, and challenges in two interrelated and timely topics of building natural language interfaces to databases and managing natural language data. The book is broken down to two major parts: (1) natural language data management and (2) natural language interfaces to databases. The first part deals with the issue of querying and managing data in natural language data sources. It reviews data models and query classes that have been either in use or under development and the storage structures that support some of theses queries. This part also reviews the issue of semantics and the developments on transforming natural language text to a meaning representation. The second part addresses the challenges surrounding building natural language interfaces to databases. It reviews the issues of understanding and translating queries expressed in natural language to database queries, the components involved in the translation, as well as models of user interactions. Finally, a range of systems are reviewed in terms of features and functions offered and the challenges addressed.

While the book covers all major ideas and techniques, to the best of our knowledge, related to the two topics, it is not intended to include an exhaustive list of works related to natural language data management and interfaces to databases, nor can it can be expected to do so given the fast-moving pace of the related fields of research in data management, natural language processing, data mining, information retrieval, and many others. However, the authors will be maintaining a web page, which will have the latest developments and progress in the areas covered in the book. If you find omissions or errors in our coverage, please do not hesitate to let us know and we will try to include them in that page and also when updating the materials in this book.

CHAPTER 2

Background

Natural language is a common type of data considered by many areas of computer science, from natural language processing to question answering. While the focus of this book is natural language within the context of databases, both as data as well as interfaces, techniques used to handling natural language in other areas of computer science are often relevant and discussed. In this chapter, we provide a brief overview of a few topics closely related to the main content of this book. The goal is not to provide a comprehensive treatment of these topics, as each of which warrants its own book, but to enable readers who are new to these topics to have enough background knowledge to better understand the terminologies and techniques discussed throughout the book. As syntactic and semantic analysis provide valuable information for natural language understanding and translation, we review them here. For syntactic analysis, we review part-of-speech tagging, morphological analysis, and syntactic and dependency parsing in Sections 2.1–2.3. This is followed by the problem of semantic parsing of natural language in Section 2.4. We then discuss the area of question answering in Section 2.6. Finally, we present an overview of dialog systems in Section 2.5. The relationships between these topics and the main topics of the book, natural language data management and natural language interfaces to databases, are discussed in more details in Chapters 3 and 4, respectively.

2.1 PART-OF-SPEECH TAGGING

Part-of-Speech tagging (also known as POS tagging) is the task of assigning each word in text to a word category such as noun, verb, and adjective. A word can take more than one part of speech, depending on its context, and a POS tagger must detect, given the context of a word, which POS tag of the word is used. While word categories vary between different languages and different tagging of even the same language, most POS taggers for English use the Penn Treebank tag set [Marcus et al., 1993], which has 45 categories. These include noun, verb, adjective, adverb, preposition (e.g., "under," "over"), determiner (e.g., "a", "the"), and conjunction (e.g., "and," "or," "but"). The four major word categories *noun, verb, adjective,* and *adverb* are considered open class, in that new words are created or added to the categories on daily basis (e.g., "to google").

It is shown that the most frequent class baseline, where each word is assigned the category it occurs the most in the training set, achieves over 90% accuracy [Jurafsky and Martin, 2009b]. This means many words are unambiguous, when it comes to POS tagging. Hidden Markov Models compute the probability of tag sequences, assigning tags based on the tags of the words before and after the target word. They are shown to achieve an accuracy close to 97% [Brants, 2000].

2.2 MORPHOLOGICAL ANALYSIS

Morphology is the study of the way words are constructed from the smallest grammatical units known as morphemes. Most words can be broken down to a central morpheme, known as stem, which gives the central meaning, and an affix, which adds to or modifies the meaning. For example, the word *teacher* can be broken down to "teach" and "er" where the latter modifies the meaning to "someone who teaches." Natural languages can be classified into three classes based on their morphological structures. In *isolating languages*, words do not change and there are no morphemes to indicate tense (e.g., past, present) or if a noun is singular or plural. Chinese Mandarin and Vietnamese are examples of this class. *Agglutinative languages* combine, morphemes including stem and affixes, with no change in their forms to express compound ideas. Table 2.1 gives an example in Turkish and Farsi. *Inflecting languages* use a single inflectional morpheme to represent multiple syntactic and semantic form or meaning.

Table 2.1: Compound nouns built using stems *khane* in Farsi and *ev* in Turksih

Farsi Compound	Turkish Compound	English Meaning
khane	ev	house
khaneha	evler	houses
khaneash	evi	his/her house
khanehayash	evleri	his/her/their houses
khaneat	evin	your house
	evden	from the house
	evlerden	from the houses
	evinden	from his/her house
	evlerinden	from his/her/their houses

A simple algorithm for morpheme segmentation, known as Morfessor, is an unsupervised method that takes as input an unannotated text corpus and produces a segmentation of the word forms in the input text [Creutz and Lagus, 2007]. The algorithm processes the word forms, one at a time. The word forms considered include the word as a whole and all possible splits of the word into substrings. The form (or split) that yields the highest probability is selected. The splitting process recursively continues until no more gain is possible. This is typically done by iteratively processing the corpus until the overall probability converges. In its first iteration over the corpus, the algorithm selects all whole words as potential morphs. Based on the observation that many word stems are mentioned as whole words as well (e.g., *ev*), the algorithm in its next iteration detects suffixes and prefixes (e.g., *ler*, *in*) by splitting long words into known stems and prefixes and suffixes. The extended set of morphs are used in the next iteration to further split the words. Improvements over this simple method are possible by considering additional features such as the categories of the morphs (e.g., prefix, stem, suffix). Supervised models further improve the accuracy of the segmentation (e.g., Durrett and DeNero [2013]).

2.3   SYNTACTIC AND DEPENDENCY PARSING

Understanding the syntactic structure of a sentence and the grammatical relationships between words plays a key role in understanding the sentence. One way to parse a sentence is to decompose it into its constituents—words or groups of words that function as a single unit or has a single role. Since phrases can be further broken down into smaller units until each unit consists of a word, this hierarchical decomposition of a sentence emits a tree called *constituency parse tree*. For example, the sentence "John teaches a course" can be broken down into a noun phrase that contains "John" and a verb phrase that has "teaches a course." The latter can further be broken down to the verb "teaches" and a noun phrase that has "a course." The phrase "a course" can be broken down to the determiner "a" and the noun "course." This parse of the sentence is shown in Figure 2.1, where the labels S, NP, VP, V, NNP, NN, and DT, respectively, denote sentence, noun phrase, verb phrase, verb, proper noun, common noun, and determiner. A sentence can have more than one parse when it is possible to generate the sentence using different production rules of the natural language grammar. This gives rise to the problem of ambiguity, which is a challenge in parsing.

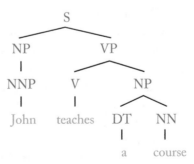

Figure 2.1: Syntactic parse of the sentence "John teaches a course."

A different approach to parsing a sentence is to only detect binary relations between words. A *dependency parse* of a sentence is a tree with each node denoting a word and each edge describing a relation. The relations may or may not be typed. When the relations are typed (e.g., subject, object, etc.), the type information is shown as edge labels in the parse tree. For example, the dependencies of the sentence "John teaches a course," can be listed as *teaches* $\xrightarrow{subj}$ *John*, *teaches* $\xrightarrow{obj}$ *course*, and *course* $\xrightarrow{det}$ *a*.

In the style of LR parsers from programming languages [Aho and Ullman, 1972], a constituency parser is generally guided by a grammar and may be implemented with a stack. As the words of a sentence are processed, they can be replaced by their categories. For example, the sentence "John teaches a course" may become "NNP V DT NN." Applying the grammar rules "NP→NNP" and "NP → DT NN" to the sequence will produce "NP V NP." This can be further transformed to "NP VP" uisng the rule "VP→V NP" and finally to "S" using the rule "S→NP VP." Putting these transformations together will give the parse tree in Figure 2.1. Multiple production rules can match a sequence, each leading to a different parse tree. In such cases, statistics from a corpus may be used to compute the likelihood of each candidate parse [Collins, 1997].

A dependency parser, on the other hand, examines the relationships between word pairs in a sentence and tags each relationship as head-to-dependent or dependent-to-head. Stanford parser [de Marneffe et al., 2006] starts with a grammar-based constituency parse of the sentence, giving the phrase structure, and identifies the head of each constituent using some rules [Collins, 2003]. Verbs and content words may be chosen as head to better describe the semantics. Once dependencies are detected, each dependency is assigned a grammatical relation type, based on the patterns given for that relation type. When there are more than one matching patterns, the pattern with the most specific grammatical relation is chosen as the dependency type.

2.4   SEMANTIC PARSING

Semantic parsing [Mooney, 2007] is the task of mapping a natural language sentence into the corresponding formal meaning representation on which a machine can act. The target output representation of meaning varies according to the task to be performed by the machines, as illustrated by examples in Figure 2.2, ranging from formal database query languages such as SQL (e.g., Zhong et al. [2017]), to procedural languages for robot control applications (e.g., Matuszek et al. [2013]), simple *intent* and *argument* structures for chatbot APIs, more general *predicate* and *argument structures* for *Semantic Role Labeling* [Jurafsky and Martin, 2009a], and more comprehensive *Abstract Meaning Representation* [Banarescu et al., 2013].

The most studied semantic parsing problem is perhaps Semantic Role Labeling (SRL) [Palmer et al., 2010a], also known as *shallow semantic parsing*. It is the task of assigning roles to each argument of each predicate in a sentence, capturing the information on "Who did what to whom, when, where, and how" expressed in a sentence. Consider the sentence in Figure 2.2d as an example. The predicate-argument structure indicates that there is an action Break, the Agent (the volitional causer of an event) of the action is John, the Theme (the participant most directly affected by an event) of the action is the window, and the Instrument used is a hammer.

Find all the publications by Michael Stonebraker

```
SELECT      P.*
FROM        Author A, Publication P
WHERE       A.AuthorID = P.AuthorID
AND         A.AuthorName = 'Michael Stonebraker'
```

(a) Formal Database Query

Go left to the end of the hall

```
(do-sequentially
   (turn-left
   (do-until
   (or
      (not
         (exists forward-loc))
      (room forward-loc))
(move-to forward-loc)))
```

(b) Robot Control Program

What is the weather tomorrow?

```
(Location: San Jose, CA, USA)
(Date: 2018-05-01)
```

(c) Chatbot API Output

John broke the window with a hammer.

```
(Predicate: Break.01)
(Agent: John)
(Theme: the window)
(Instrument: a hammer)
```

(d) Semantic Role Labeling

The boy did not go.

```
(p / possible
   :domain (g / go-01
         :arg0 (b / boy))
   :polarity -))
```

(e) Abstract Meaning Representation

Figure 2.2: Example meaning representations for semantic parsing for different tasks.

The predicate-argument structures help to capture syntactically different sentences with the same semantics in a uniform way. For instance, the same structure in Figure 2.2d applies to all the sentences below despite of their syntactic differences.

- `The window was broken by John with a hammer.`

- `With a hammer, the window was broken by John.`

- `With a hammer, John broke the window.`

- `John, with a hammer, broke the window.`

The task of SRL is generally treated as a supervised machine learning task, with models trained on labeled corpora such as PropBank [Palmer et al., 2005] or FrameNet [Baker et al., 1998]. Algorithms generally start by tokenizing and parsing a sentence into a dependency parse tree and then automatically tagging each parse tree node with a semantic role. Some recent work (e.g., He et al. [2017b], Zhou and Xu [2015]) has successfully leveraged deep neural network to perform end-to-end learning of semantic role labeling without parsing. Semantic role labeling is further discussed in the context of transforming natural language text in Section 3.6.

2.5   QUESTION ANSWERING

Question answering (QA) is the task of automatically answering questions posed by humans in a natural language. Based on the source of their answers, QA systems can be divided into two paradigms: *IR-based question answering* and *knowledge-based question answering*.

IR-based question answering relies on information available in unstructured data such as text on the Web or in specialized collections such as PubMed. Given a user question, a typical IR-based question answering system first classifies the question based on the likely answer type (e.g., who, where, when) and formulates queries to send to a search engine. The search engine returns ranked passages. Finally, the system extracts candidate answers from the passages and returns ranked answers.

Knowledge-based question answering relies on information available in a structured knowledge base. The knowledge base could consist of triples of simple relations, or more complex structured data such as a relational or graph database. Given a user question, a knowledge-based question answering system usually first translates it into a structured query (e.g., a logical expressions or a SQL query) and executes the translated query over the knowledge base to retrieve answers, potentially after re-ranking, to the original question.

Classic QA systems are usually IR-based, as such systems are easier to build with lower upfront cost. Real-world QA systems such as the DeepQA system [Ferrucci, 2010] in IBM's Watson generally are hybrid systems, using a combination of text datasets and structured knowledge bases to answer questions. As an example, DeepQA extracts a wide variety of meanings from the question (syntactic parses, relations, named entities, ontological information), and then finds large numbers of candidate answers from both structured knowledge bases and unstructured text such as Wikipedia and newspaper articles. Each candidate answer is then reasoned and is scored before being ranked based on its score.

Recent advances in the area of computer vision has expanded the interest in and the scope of question answering beyond text. Increasing number of works attempt to support visual question answering [Teney et al., 2017] as well as multimodal question answering [Li et al., 2017].

2.6   DIALOG SYSTEM

A *dialog system*, also known as *conversational agent*, is a computer program that can interact with a human in a natural and coherent turn-to-turn structure. Figure 2.3 depicts the basic architecture of a dialog system. As can be seen, a typical dialog system consists of the following major components.

1. *Input Recognition*: The input to a dialog system by a user could be human voice, gesture, or handwriting. This component recognizes such signals and translates them into natural language text.

2. *Language Understanding*: This component interprets the recognized natural language input from the user into a semantic representation. The understanding typically involves a variety of natural language processing techniques including named entity recognition, part-of-speech tagging, syntactic parsing, and semantic parsing. The (Language Understanding) analysis of the current dialog acts may depend on the history and the state of the dialog maintained by the Dialog Manager.

3. *Dialog Manager*: This component keeps the history and the state of the dialog and manages the general flow of the conversation. It analyzes the semantic representation of the user's input and passes it to the Task Manager and then takes the output of the Task Manager and passes it to Response Generation. The structure of the dialog could be managed as predefined finite state transducers (e.g., Figure 2.4), frames (e.g., Figure 2.5), classic AI plans, and information states in models learned by deep neural networks.

4. *Task Manager*: Based on the input from the Dialog Manager, this components decides the system dialog act based on the specific task domain. For instance, for the airline booking dialog system as illustrated in Figure 2.4, the Task Manager is responsible for booking the ticket based on the information provided by a user via dialog.

5. *Response Generation*: This component generates the response to the user in the current dialog.

6. *Output Rendering*: Finally, This component renders the system response into an appropriate format (e.g., voice, robotic act) to communicate to the user.

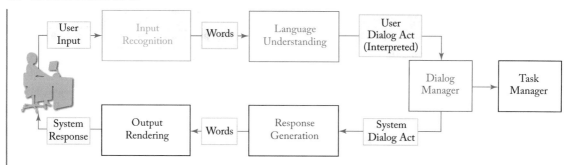

Figure 2.3: Basic components of a dialog system.

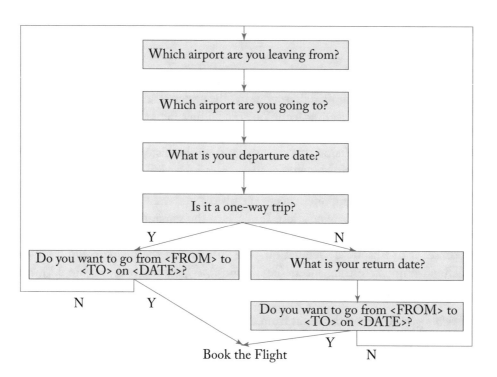

Figure 2.4: Example finite state dialog manager.

Slot	Question
ORIGIN_AIRPORT	Which airport are you leaving from?
DESTINATION_CITY	Which airport are you going to?
DEPARTURE_DATE	When would you like to leave?
RETURN_DATE	When would you like to return?

Figure 2.5: Example of a frame-based dialog manager.

Dialog systems with text-only interfaces (e.g., a chat bot) only need components (2)–(5). We refer readers to the relevant literature [Jokinen and McTear, 2010, Jurafsky and Martin, 2009a] for a more comprehensive overview of dialog systems, particularly speech dialog systems.

CHAPTER 3

Natural Language Data Management

3.1 OVERVIEW

Long before the invention of modern computers and the formation of computer science as a discipline, natural languages have been used to record observations, to describe entities and relationships and to exchange information. Compared to more formal languages and abstractions such as formal logic, relational model, XML, RDF, etc., natural languages clearly are not the best medium for representing data and expressing facts and relationships about real-world entities. However, the truth of the matter is that much of human knowledge and everyday information is written and communicated in some form of natural language. Furthermore, the advent of the Web and the wide-spread digitization and content sharing over the Internet has made a huge volume of natural language data, initially intended for human consumption, available for almost all users. Managing such content, governed by a natural language grammar, is a challenge in terms of efficient and effective querying. Traditionally this data has been stored outside databases and has been processed using natural language processing tools and Information Retrieval (IR) engines, in isolation from other data sources. However, IR engines are very limited in their querying functionality and the issues of efficient storage and querying are not addressed within natural language processing systems. Also, there are many scenarios where natural language text co-exists and is queried with more structured data. Here are some scenarios.

- We have the financial filings of a company (e.g., as shown in Figure 3.1) and want to find evidence that supports or contradicts a claim. U.S. Securities and Exchange Commission,[1] which collects such reports on regular basis, currently provides access to more than 21 million filings.

- We have a collection of medical articles and want to find treatments for a disease and their success rates as reported in those articles.

- We are given the health records of a set of patients who have gone under a surgery and want to find post-operative complications as reported in the patient records.

---

[1]https://www.sec.gov/edgar/searchedgar/companysearch.html

- We have a few candidates running in a federal election and want to gauge the degree of support they are getting in social media (e.g., Twitter) and the contexts in which their names are mentioned.

- We are retrieving products that satisfy some user needs (e.g., from relational tables) and want to include some statistics or analyses of each product based on the sentiments of online reviews.

> ... At March 31, 2017, we had approximately $9.0 billion carrying value (including hedge accounting fair value adjustments) of senior unsecured notes outstanding; no indebtedness outstanding under our up to $1.5 billion commercial paper program; no indebtedness outstanding under our $2.0 billion senior unsecured revolving credit facility and $2.0 billion of available borrowing capacity (subject to customary conditions to borrowing) under our senior unsecured revolving credit facility (of which $1.5 billion of available borrowing capacity was reserved to provide liquidity support, if required , for our commercial paper program); and no secured indebtedness outstanding. At March 31, 2017, our subsidiaries had approximately $12.2 million of indebtedness outstanding. ...

Figure 3.1: A filing at U.S. Securities and Exchange Commission.

A unifying theme in all these scenarios is that (1) text sources are queried and analyzed in granularities smaller than a document, and (2) text sources are queried in conjunction with more structured data which may be available either as meta-data of the same text sources (e.g., the poster of a tweet, the date it is posted, the user who retweeted it, etc.) or from different sources (e.g., the names of candidates and their parties). There is a large range of applications with the same or similar data requirements that can benefit from a possible integrated solution. In general, IR approaches are less useful when text is queried in small granularities such as a sentence or is joined with structured data; hence, a viable choice is to manage and query the data at some abstraction level (e.g., sentences) in a database, allowing easy development of more complex applications. However, there are two major challenges that hinder this development: (1) many relational database systems currently lack support for querying natural language data and (2) the problem of transforming natural language text to a meaning representation that can be easily queried, aggregated, and joined with other sources is not well resolved.[2]

This chapter reviews the latest progress in the area of natural language data management and some of the principles that have allowed this progress as well as a discussion of the challenges. The organization of the rest of the chapter is as follows. Section 3.2 reviews some of

---

[2]Other challenges that arise include variations in entity naming and referencing and differences due to synonyms and paraphrasing, text formatting, misspelling, etc. These challenges are out of the scope of this book and are addressed elsewhere (e.g., Christen [2012a], Lin and Pantel [2001], Lin et al. [2003].)

the sources that generate natural language data. Data models and queries are discussed in Sections 3.3 and 3.4, and strategies for efficiently supporting queries over natural language text are discussed in Section 3.5. The problem of transforming natural language text to a meaning representation that can be easily queried is discussed in Section 3.6.

3.2   DATA SOURCES

A challenge in querying natural languages is that the data may come from different sources and those sources can vary in (1) the quality of the data they offer, (2) the language of encoding, and (3) the medium or format of the storage. Querying natural language data is intertwined with understanding these challenges as well as the areas and the sources where the challenges are either easier to overcome or can be avoided.

Quality. News articles have been a more traditional source of content and have also been used in training many early NLP tools (e.g., Aone et al. 1998, Collins 1996, Lin and Pantel 2001). The quality of data in news articles may depend on the authority of the sources and the type of the articles. Data from more authoritative sources (e.g., court documents, financial statement filings, and well-respected news sites) is expected to be more accurate simply because the sources don't want to jeopardize the trust conferred on them by the public. At the same time, some authoritative sources such as news sites may publish opinion columns, and these columns can have less factual content or be less accurate than news articles. The web pages, on the other hand, are more diverse; some pages are rich with more factual statements, and are often well-edited, such as Wikipedia pages and scientific articles. These pages may also be well-written since they often go through an editorial review. In contrast, many pages go through very least to none editorial reviews and can publish opinions or statements that are hard to verify.

Language. The language of encoding may determine the ease at which the content can be parsed, queried and analyzed. In terms of the resources that one needs to understand the encoding of the content, English by far is the most resourceful language. Some of these resources include large parsed corpora, aka treebanks (e.g., Penn Treebank [Marcus et al., 1993] and MASC [Resource, 2017]), n-grams (e.g., Lin et al. [2012] and Norvig [2017]), parsers and part-of-speech taggers (e.g., Stanford toolkit [Manning et al., 2014]), etc. Some resources that may help in understanding the content (e.g., Wikipedia) are available in multiple languages but the English version is usually more comprehensive or accurate. For the same reason, in multilingual shared tasks, English usually tops the list in terms of the accuracy of the results (e.g., Tjong Kim Sang and De Meulder [2003]).

Medium. Natural language data can be in the form of text or speech. Many customer call recordings are in the form of speech; to analyze such data using text processing tools, recordings are often transcribed into text. The process involves audio sampling and feature extraction to recognize individual sounds and to convert them to text. Despite the recent progress in this area, transcription error cannot be avoided. However, the error has been reduced in recent years; Google has reported reaching an 8% error rate [Pichai, 2015].

Without loss of generality, our discussion in this chapter will focus on textual data in English.

3.3   DATA MODELS

Intended for human consumption, natural language content generally does not lend itself to an easily recognizable or a non-ambiguous data model. On the other hand, one needs some sort of a data model for querying the content. There are two general approaches that may be used to establish a structure over content and to allow the relationships to be parsed: (1) interpreting context as schema and (2) mapping natural language text to more formal models.

3.3.1   INTERPRETING CONTEXT AS SCHEMA

Often users know the context where facts and relationships are expressed, and those contexts can be used as clues in querying. For example, consider the lease agreement template in Figure 3.2; a user who is searching for a list of lessors, lessees, and the address of the property being leased may use phrases such as "as lessor," "as lessee," and "located at" to detect field boundaries and to extract the relationships. It can be noted that there is no clear separation between the schema description and the data instance, and it is up to the queries or applications to make this distinction.

> *<Name of Lessor>*, as Lessor, does hereby agree to let to *<Name of Lessee>*, as Lessee, a parking space located at *<Street Address of Parking Space>* (Building/Street Address) *<City of Parking Space>* (City), *<State of Parking Space>* (State) , such parking space being further described Parking Space No. *<Parking Space Number>* at the aforementioned location. The following terms and conditions shall apply to this Parking Space Lease Agreement ("Agreement"):
> Terms and Conditions: ...

Figure 3.2: Parking space lease agreement (source: http://www.docracy.com/3241/parking-space-lease-agreement).

3.3.2   MAPPING CONTENT TO MORE FORMAL MODELS

Natural language text may be transformed into a formal representation that describes the syntactic and the semantic structure of a sentence and the relationships between tokens, and these models may be treated as a data model. Consider the parse tree of the sentence "Edmonton with a population of 928,000 is the capital of Alberta," as shown in Figure 3.3. Even though this is only a syntactic annotation of the sentence, the tags and their relationships in the tree provide some means of querying the data. For example, the listing of the terms "Edmonton," "population," and "928,000" in the same subtree indicates a relationship that may be queried or analyzed. Similarly the relationship between Alberta and its capital may be queried using the dependencies between the terms "Edmonton," "capital," and "Alberta," as shown in Figure 3.4.

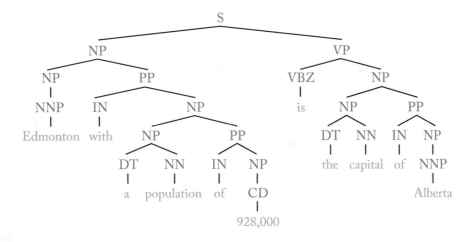

Figure 3.3: Syntactic parse tree.

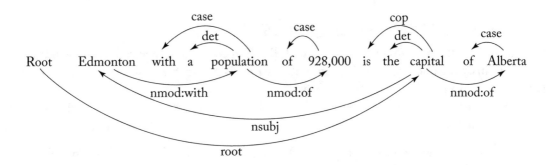

Figure 3.4: Dependency parse tree.

A natural language sentence may also be decomposed into a set of formal statements, aka frames, where the meaning is established by connecting the components or frames to encyclopedic knowledge. For example, the sentence "Edmonton with a population of 928,000 is the capital of Alberta," can be broken into two frames "population" and "capital" and those frames may be linked to an ontology (e.g., dbpedia) in the sense that the meaning of each frame relates to and is defined in terms of all the world knowledge that are linked to the same frame in the ontology. Modeling a sentence as a frame graph links language internal and external information, providing a powerful model for representing the meaning. As an example, Table 3.1 gives core and non-core roles of the frame *receiving*, as listed in FrameNet [Baker et al., 1998], and here is an example sentence labeled with those roles:

(Ullman)$_{Recipient}$ received (the SIGMOD contribution award)$_{Theme}$ (in 1996)$_{Time}$.

Transforming natural language text to a meaning representation (aka semantic parsing) is further discussed in Section 3.6.

Table 3.1: Roles of the frame *receiving* listed in FrameNet

Core	Donor, Recipient, Theme
Non-Core	Countertransfer, Depictive, Manner, Means, Mode of Transfer, Path, Place, Purpose_of_theme, Role, Time

3.4   QUERIES

Natural language content may be queried in the source format without deep analysis or understanding. This section reviews a few such query classes that have been developed. Some of these classes (e.g., Boolean queries) operate at the level of text with no analysis while others (e.g., tree pattern queries) rely on some syntactic analysis such as parsing.

3.4.1   BOOLEAN KEYWORD QUERIES

If we treat natural language content as free text, Boolean queries may be used to find windows of text that satisfy the queries. Variations in syntax, which is common in natural language content, can be easily expressed in the form of disjunctions. Queries may as well include wild cards to allow even more variations to be expressed easily. Here is a query from TREC legal track[3] for finding documents that discuss the placement of tobacco products in G-rated movies:

((guide! OR strateg! OR approv!) AND (place! or promot!)) AND (("G-rated" OR "G rated" OR family) W/5 (movie! OR film! OR picture!))

The use of a wild card at the end of the term "strateg" includes different formattings of the term (such as strategy, strategies, and strategic) in search without explicitly listing them. A Boolean query may also place some constraint on the length of a matching window, as done for the terms "family" and "movie" in the given query where their mentions cannot be more than five words apart.

On the other hand, natural language text is usually broken down into smaller logical units such as article, section, paragraph, and sentence and queries can have matches at any of those levels of granularities. Quicklaw and Westlaw, which use Boolean queries as their default search,

---

[3]https://trec-legal.umiacs.umd.edu/

allow searches to be constrained to some of these units. For example, the query "text /S database" in Quicklaw[4] finds articles that have the given terms in a sentence.

3.4.2   GRAMMAR-BASED SEARCHES

Natural language text is expected to follow some generative grammar rules, and those rules may be treated as schema for querying. A caveat is that grammar rules for natural language text are often complex, and a query formulation is generally less straightforward. Hence, grammar-based searches are well-suited for more structured text. For example, bibliographic records in a document can be broken down into entries such as author, title, publication venue, year, and page numbers and the ordering of the entries and their composition in a record may be described using some rules, which may in turn be used in queries to parse the input. Grammar-based queries are used in the context of text databases for searching bibliographic records and dictionary entries [Gonnet and Tompa, 1987] as well as for querying semi-structured documents [Abiteboul et al., 1997, Christophides et al., 1994]. For example, the following SQL-like query [Christophides et al., 1994] finds sections of articles that contain "natural language data."

```
select ss
from a in Articles, s in a.sections, ss in s.subsectns
where text(ss) contains (''natural language data'')
```

3.4.3   TEXT PATTERN QUERIES

Often the user knows the context where a desired answer is expected and may use this context to find the answers. For example, consider searching for mentions of hockey players affiliated with Edmonton Oilers in text; one context where such a name can be mentioned is "Oilers player NAME" where the name follows the phrase "Edmonton Oilers." These contexts may be expressed as text patterns with some wild cards to allow variations and some tags to mark the location(s) where an answer is expected. Unlike regular expressions, commonly used in programming and shell scripting languages and in SQL, the grouping operators and the wild cards in a text pattern may not be expressed at the level of single characters.

DeWild [Rafiei and Li, 2009a,b] introduces two wild cards in text pattern queries. A percentage sign indicates one or more noun phrases, and each noun phrase can consist of one or more terms. The wild card, when used in a query, indicates the location of a noun phrase or noun phrases that must be extracted. For example, the query "*Oilers players such as %*" will extract noun phrases *Andrew Ference* and *Connor McDavid* from text "He was impressed by the efforts from the Oilers players such as Andrew Ference and Connor McDavid." A star denotes a set of terms or phrases that have a similar meaning to a given phrase. Consider again searching for oilers players. The query "*Oilers players such as %*" will not retrieve players who are referred to as "forwards," "defensemen," or "stars." To include those terms in the search, the query may be

---

changed to "*Oilers *players* such as %*" where the term inside the stars not only matches "players" but also its synonyms such as "forward," "defenseman," "shooter," "lineman," etc.[5] Table 3.2 gives some examples of text pattern queries.

Table 3.2: Examples of text pattern queries

Natural Language Question	Text Pattern Query
Who invented the light bulb?	% invented the light bulb
What does Canada consist of?	Canada consists of %
Where is Glacier National Park?	Gracier National Park is located in %
Which states border California?	California is bordered by % & % is U.S. state

In a language similar to DeWild, IKE [Dalvi et al., 2016] supports text patterns over surface text and POS tags of sentences. IKE also allows matches over distributional similar words and the maximum number of those words is specified in queries. For example, the pattern dog~10 will match the term "dog" and any of its 10 synonyms.

A challenge in using text patterns for querying natural language text is the possibility of a mismatch between the expressions of queries and texts that have the relevant information. Although using wild cards allows more expressive queries, a fact can still be potentially expressed in different contexts and a query that gives one context can miss many qualified candidates. For example, the query "*Oilers *players* such as %*" will not match the texts "... Oilers player Andrew Ference ..." or "... Andrew Ference has been playing for Oilers ...." DeWild introduces rewriting rules or transformations to express the relationships between alternative query expressions. Some of these transformations are quite general and include hyponym patterns (as shown in Table 3.3) and morphological variations. DeWild uses a datalog-[Ceri et al., 1989]style rewriting rule language to express the transformations between text patterns. Here is part of those rewritings for hyponym patterns.

```
(.+) is an? (.+)
->
$2 such as $1 && plural($2)
$1, and other $2 && plural($1)
$1, a $2 && singular($2)
```

Keywords from queries may be remembered using *capturing groups* (marked by parentheses) on the left side of a rule and may be recalled on the right side using back references (e.g., $1 and $2). The remembered values may be transformed (e.g., to plural or singular forms) before

---

[5]The set of synonyms of a term may be obtained from a thesaurus or be constructed using a corpus, based on the distributional similarity of the terms [Lin et al., 2003, Qu et al., 2017]. Also, see Section 3.6.3 for more details.

Table 3.3: Hyponym patterns (reported by Hearst [1992])

NP2 is a(n) NP1
NP1 (,) such as NP2List
such NP1 as NP2List
NP1 (,) especially NP2List
NP1 (,) including NP2List
NP2List and other NP1
NP2List and other NP1
NP2, a(n) NP1
NP1 NP2

constructing a rewrite. The given rewriting, when applied to "Canada is a country" will produce the following three rewrites: "countries such as Canada," "Canada, and other countries," and "Canada, a country."

3.4.4   TREE PATTERN QUERIES

Text pattern queries can fail in the presence of additional terms in a matching text. For example, the query "Oilers forward %" will not match the text "Oilers star forward Leon Draisaitl" because of the adjective "star" in text but not in the query. Variations due to optional terms such as adjectives may be expressed in queries but this has two side-effects: (1) the query can become more complex and (2) it is easy to miss some of the variations. An alternative approach is to treat both text and queries as collections of syntactically annotated trees.

More concretely, syntactic relationships between terms in a sentence can be modeled as an unranked node-labeled tree (cf. Section 3.3.2). Since the tree is unranked, each node can have an arbitrary number of children. Queries over syntactic annotated trees are modeled as trees with nodes representing the terms and annotations to be matched and the edges describing binary relationships between the terms or annotations. Tree pattern queries may be generated from natural language questions, following the same process used for parsing text. This is desirable in many cases especially when the user is not familiar with the grammar, the annotations, or the tree syntax. Tree pattern queries may also be composed by expert users who are well-versed in the language syntax. Figure 3.5 gives an example tree pattern query in the form of a constituency parse tree, and Figure 3.6 does the same in the form of a dependency parse tree. These queries may be posed over the tree pattern queries in Figures 3.3 and 3.4, respectively.

It is not hard to see that two or more children of a query node can have the same labels, for example, when two adjectives are modifying a single noun. Hence, we may require that query

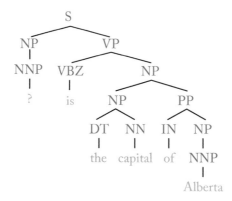

Figure 3.5: A query as a syntactic parse tree.

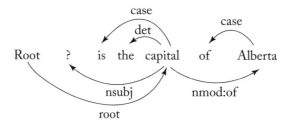

Figure 3.6: A query as a dependency parse tree.

nodes with the same labels must match different data nodes or the matching to be an injective function.

3.4.5   COMBINING TEXT AND TREE PATTERN QUERIES

Text and tree patterns may be combined to express conditions on both surface text of a sentence and the syntactic relationships tagged by a parser. Koko [Wang et al., 2018] supports conditions on both surface text and the dependency tree structure of matching sentences. A query in Koko can consist of three clauses. An *extract* clause is where the variables are defined, including those to be extracted. The extract clause also lists all conditions on the types and the dependency relationships of the matching tokens that must be satisfied. A *satisfying* clause is where a score is computed for each match, as an aggregation of the scores from all matching sentences, and a threshold on the matches may be specified. An *excluding* clause may also be given to list any matches that should not be returned.

3.4.6 SUMMARY

Unlike Boolean and grammar-based searches where the query result is a set of matching documents, the result of text-pattern and tree-pattern queries are terms or phrases for unary queries or tuples consisting of terms and phrases for n-ary queries. Supporting word level extractions is important for several reasons. First, a large class of natural language questions, referred to as factoid questions, can easily be expressed as one or more text pattern or tree pattern queries (see Table 3.2 for some examples). Second, text and tree pattern queries can be easily joined with each other or with the data residing in a database, allowing the formulation of more expressive queries. For example, knowing that the result of a text or tree pattern query is a city name, the result may be refined by looking up the values in a database table populated with city names.

3.5   INDEXING NATURAL LANGUAGE TEXT

Indexes are crucial for efficiently supporting queries over large text collections. These indexes are constructed once and are used to evaluate many queries, hence their amortized construction cost is negligible. Also, the construction is often done offline and it does not affect the cost of online queries.

A common approach for efficiently storing and accessing text (and not necessarily natural language text) has been to build an inverted index of words and to provide a fast access to their frequency, location, etc. However, an inverted index provides only a limited support for many natural language processing tasks. For example, an inverted index can reduce the search space of text pattern and tree pattern queries by directing the search to sentences that mention some of the query terms, but the number of such sentences can be large if the query terms are not selective enough. Major querying systems over syntactically annotated parsed corpora, such as TGrep2 [Rhode] and CorpusSearch [Randall, 2018], require an in-memory scan of the entire corpus for answering any single query; these systems can benefit from more efficient storage options. We next present storage and index structures for efficiently supporting text pattern and tree pattern queries.

3.5.1   INDEXING FOR TEXT PATTERN QUERIES

There are a few indexing strategies that are applicable and may be used to speed up text pattern queries.

Inverted Index

Text pattern queries may be evaluated using an inverted index, and an evaluation strategy can be adapted from those developed for phrase and multi-keyword queries. Given a corpus to be searched, suppose each word is indexed and the posting list of a term includes the ids of documents and sentences that contain the term and the term offsets (as shown in Table 3.4). Given a text pattern query, one can intersect the posting lists of the terms in the query and verify their offsets to find sentences that contain the terms in the given order. The matching sentences can then be retrieved and the desired parts (e.g., those matching the wild card %) can be extracted. A downside of using an inverted index is long posting lists; this is an issue for text pattern queries since frequent terms such as "is," "a," and "the" are commonly used in these queries (see Section 3.4.3 for examples).

Table 3.4: Words and their postings, extracted from the text "Edmonton is the capital of Alberta. The city population is 928,000" assuming the document id is 1.

Word	Posting List
edmonton	(1, 1, 1)
is	(1, 1,2), (1, 2,4)
the	(1, 1,3),(1, 2,1)
capital	(1, 1,4)
of	(1, 1,5)
alberta	(1, 1,6)
city	(1, 2,2)
population	(1, 2,3)
928,000	(1, 2,5)

Neighbor Index

This is an inverted index that stores for each term both the left and the right neighbor terms and may better suit queries over natural language text [Cafarella and Etzioni, 2005]. Storing the neighboring terms can improve the performance of text pattern queries since terms matching the wild cards are stored in the index. For example, the posting list of the term "player" will have the matching terms for the query *Oilers player %*, assuming that the nouns are tagged and stored as neighbors. This improvement comes at the cost of a significant increase in index size.

Word Permuterm Index

Word permuterm index [Chubak and Rafiei, 2010] is an adaptation of Garfield's elegant Permuterm index [Garfield, 1976] for natural language text applications. In particular, it has been shown to perform well for text pattern queries. The index has three components: (1) a word-level Burrows-Wheeler Transformation (BWT) of text, (2) a mechanism to efficiently store and access the alphabet, and (3) a mechanism to efficiently access the ranks.

A word-level BWT of the text is obtained by (1) finding all word-level cyclic rotations of text, (2) sorting the rotations, and (3) taking the vector of last words from the sorted set of rotations in Step 2. Let's denote this vector with L. Consider the text $T = $ *Paris is a city in*

Europe $ European cities such as Paris $~ with two sentences and the symbols $ and ~, respectively, marking the sentence boundaries and the end of text. The set of all rotations of T, as shown in Figure 3.7, gives L.

i	Permutation	L
1	$ European cities such as Paris $ ~ $ Paris is a city in	Europe
2	$ Paris is a city in Europe $ European cities such as Paris $	~
3	$ ~ $ Paris is a city in Europe $ European cities such as	Paris
4	Europe $ European cities such as Paris $ ~ $ Paris is a city	in
5	European cities such as Paris $ ~ $ Paris is a city in Europe	$
6	Paris $ ~ $ Paris is a city in Europe $ European cities such	as
7	Paris is a city in Europe $ European cities such as Paris $~	$
8	a city in Europe $ European cities such as Paris $ ~ $ Paris	is
9	as Paris $ ~ $ Paris is a city in Europe $ European cities	such
10	cities such as Paris $ ~ $ Paris is a city in Europe $	European
11	city in Europe $ European cities such as Paris $ ~ $ Paris is	a
12	in Europe $ European cities such as Paris $ ~ $ Paris is a	city
13	is a city in Europe $ European cities such as Paris $ ~ $	Paris
14	such as Paris $ ~ $ Paris is a city in Europe $ European	cities
15	~ $ Paris is a city in Europe $ European cities such as Paris	$

Figure 3.7: Sorted permutations of T with the last word vector L marked.

BWT has some interesting properties; in particular, one property that is relevant to text pattern queries is that the text can be traversed backward using L. More precisely, given the term at index i of L, i.e., $L[i]$, the index of the term on the left of $L[i]$ in T is

$$LF(i) = C(L[i]) + Rank_{L[i]}(L, i),$$

where $C(L[i])$ is the number of words that are lexicographically smaller than $L[i]$ and $Rank_{L[i]}(L, i)$ is the number of times $L[i]$ appears in the sub-sequence $L[1 \ldots i]$. In other words, $LF(i)$ indicates where the term preceding $L[i]$ in T is located in L. For example, $LF(8) = C['is'] + Rank_{'is'}(L, 8) = 12 + 1 = 13$, and $L[13]$ is 'Paris,' which is the term preceding $L[8] =' is'$ in T.

To efficiently support backward traversals over text, one needs efficient implementations of functions $C()$ and $Rank()$. C can be implemented as a dictionary, maintaining for each term both its frequency and its cumulative frequency in the lexicographical ordering of the terms. The dictionary, implemented as a hash, can give constant-time access to $C(t)$, the number of terms that are smaller than term t. Naive implementations of *Rank* with alphabet Σ over a text of size n requires $O(n)$ time and space when rank is computed each time from scratch by scanning L, and $O(1)$ time and $O(n|\Sigma|)$ space when rank is fully computed in advance. Chubak and Rafiei show that rank can be computed using a succinct data structure such as the Wavelet tree [Grossi et al., 2003] and this reduces the search time to $O(log|\Sigma|)$. More details about Word Permuterm index and its properties and performance can be found in the literature [Chubak and Rafiei, 2010].

Using a word permuterm index, text pattern queries may be traversed from right to left using the terms that are present or are retrieved in previous traversals. A right-to-left traversal is useful when the query has its salient terms on the right and maybe the wild cards on the left. Since we are not expecting all text pattern queries to follow this structure, it is desirable to construct another word permuterm index that allows a left-to-right traversal of text. This can be easily done by simply reversing the order of the terms in text (i.e., making the first term as last, the second term as the second last, etc.) before constructing the word permuterm index.

3.5.2   INDEXING FOR TREE PATTERN QUERIES

Given a tree pattern query Q and a node-labeled data tree T, we say T matches Q if there exists a mapping function f such that (1) f maps every node of Q to a node of T, and (2) if there is an edge between query nodes u and v, then there is an edge between $f(u)$ and $f(v)$ in T. The mapping function may be injective to enforce that every query node maps to a different data node, as discussed in Section 3.4.5. Irrespective of how data trees are generated from natural language text (e.g., using automated tools such as syntactic parsers or manually) and the specifics of the mapping function, the question being studied here is how data trees can be structured and stored such that queries can be answered efficiently.

One simple strategy for indexing syntactically annotated trees is to keep some structural information for each node. For example, LPath [Bird et al., 2006] keeps for each node its interval coding, which allows checking for containment and adjacency relationships. Koko [Wang et al., 2018] constructs an inverted index on the parse labels of all dependency paths starting from the root. For example, the posting list of the path "/Root" includes tokens that sit under the root node in the dependency trees of all sentences. For our dependency tree in Figure 3.4, the posting list of "/Root" will include the token "capital" and that of "/Root/nsubj" will include "Edmonton." The posting list may include additional information that can help with finding matches, such as sentence id, the word offset, and the depth of the token in the dependency tree.

With nodes (or paths) of data trees stored in an index, the search for matching trees becomes the problem of finding a set of nodes (or paths) that match the query in their labels and are in the same parent-child relationships as their matching query nodes.

There is a large body of work on indexing and querying general trees and graphs that may also be applied to syntactic annotated trees. For example, ATreeGrep [Shasha et al., 2002] stores all paths of a collection of trees into a suffix array and uses a hash index of nodes and edges to prune candidates. However, there are two issues with these approaches. First, a general tree indexing approach will not be aware of the properties of the sources from which the syntactic annotated trees are generated and may not be efficient or comparable to algorithms that use this information. Second, the matching function may not support the kind of mapping that is desired in natural language contexts. For example, ATreeGrep, a competitive algorithm for matching unordered labeled trees, does not support injective matching. On the other hand, injective matching of syntactic annotated trees can be important, as discussed in Section 3.4.4. In the rest of this section, we discuss, in more detail, an index that is specifically developed for syntactic annotated trees.

Subtree Index

Given a set S of syntactically annotated trees and a size parameter mss, consider the set of all unique subtrees of sizes $1, 2, \ldots, mss$ that can be extracted from the trees in S, and associate to each subtree a posting list that includes the ids of all trees in S where the subtree appears. Figure 3.8 gives an example where unique subtrees of sizes 2 and 3 are extracted as keys. Syntactic annotated tree are unordered and so are their subtrees; this reduces the number of unique keys that are extracted. However, the number of unique subtrees in general can be extremely large; given alphabet Σ of node labels and a subtree template of size s, the number of unique subtrees that can be constructed is $O(|\Sigma|^s)$. Chubak and Rafiei [2012] experimentally show that the number of unique subtrees in a corpus of news articles grows almost linearly with the input corpus size. A reason for this is that similar structures are plentiful in a corpus of parsed trees, simply because there is a small set of grammatical structures that are commonly used in natural language text; the number of such unique trees does not grow dramatically even considering differences in writing styles, grammatical deviations, etc.

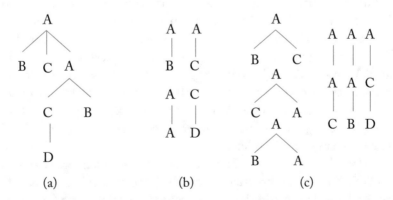

Figure 3.8: Computing index keys: (a) input tree, index keys of sizes (b) 2 and (c) 3.

Also, the size of the posting list grows with the number of subtrees that can be extracted from a tree. This number ranges from $n - m + 1$ to $\binom{n-1}{m-1}$ for a tree of size n and subtrees of size

m. The lower bound is for the case where the branching factor is 1 and the tree forms a branch of height n. The upper bound is for the case where the tree has a root with $n - 1$ children. Clearly the number of postings grows dramatically with n and m. Again it is shown that nodes with large branching factors are not that common in natural language text. In one experiment [Chubak and Rafiei, 2012], the average branching factor of internal nodes is reported to be 1.52. Hence the number of subtrees is quite manageable for small values of m (e.g., for m less than 6).

Summarizing these results, the number of unique keys and the posting list sizes can both be quite large for general trees and this is a deterrent when indexing using subtrees as keys. However, annotated parse trees behave quite well in terms of the number of unique keys and the sizes of the posting lists, and this makes them good candidates as index keys. Next, we discuss how these keys can stored and retrieved.

Coding Subtrees

With each syntactically annotated tree decomposed into a set of subtrees of size mss or less, those subtrees need to be flattened with the structural information encoded to allow a fast pruning at query time. There are a number of encoding schemes that may be used.

One basic coding scheme, referred to as *filter-based coding*, is to keep for each subtree only a reference to where the subtree appears. The coding scheme does not maintain any structural information about the trees or the position of the subtrees. The posting list of a subtree stores, similar to any inverted index, a sorted list of unique tree ids that contain the subtree.

Subtree interval coding generalizes the interval coding commonly used for XML documents and assigns to each node a pair of *pre* and *post* numbers indicating the pre- and post-visit ranks of the node in a Depth-First Search (DFS) traversal, respectively. A level number is typically maintained to handle parent child queries. Also, the order of a node in a pre-order traversal may be stored to differentiate the instances of symmetric postings stored under the same index keys. It can be noted that subtree interval coding keeps structural information that is important for pruning. For example, given the tree in Figure 3.8a as a query and the posting lists of the subtrees A(B)(C)(A) and A(C(D))(B), one can join the posting lists to enforce the parent-child relationships between the two subtrees and only retrieve trees that match the query. This benefit comes at a cost of some storage overhead. The size of an index built using a subtree interval coding can be 2–5 times larger than that of a filter-based coding for mss ranging from 1–5; the gap becomes larger for larger values of mss.

Root-split interval coding aims at offering the best of both filter-based and subtree interval coding schemes with the idea of representing each subtree as concisely as possible. Root split coding stores for each subtree, in addition to the tree identifier, only the (pre, post, level) values of its root. Compared to subtree interval coding, this simple strategy reduces the posting list size of a subtree of size m by a factor of at least m. A question now is if this concise encoding has sufficient information to allow joining the posting lists of query subtrees. The answer is affirmative but the queries cannot be arbitrarily decomposed and joined since the structural information is not kept for all nodes. One decomposition under which this join is possible is *root-split cover*.

Definition 3.1   Given a query Q and a set $C = \{c_1, \ldots, c_k\}$ of subtrees that cover Q (i.e., every node and edge of Q is listed in some tree in C), then C is a root-split cover of Q if and only if either $C = \{Q\}$ or for every subtree c_i, there exists a subtree c_j, $1 \leq i, j \leq k$, such that one of the following holds: (1) both c_i and c_j have the same root in Q, (2) the root of c_i is the parent of c_j in Q, or (3) the root of c_j is the parent of c_i in Q.

Less formally, a root-split cover is a cover that can be evaluated only by performing joins over the roots of its subtrees. Such a cover is useful for root-split coding since the coding scheme only stores the structural information about the root node of each index key. It can be noted that, every query Q has at least one valid root-split cover, which is the set containing individual nodes of Q, though this composition may not be efficient. Next, we discuss how a "better" query decomposition can be obtained.

Query Decomposition

Given a query Q, an efficient query plan can be selected by (1) finding a "good" set of subtrees that cover Q and serve as data streams placed at the leaves of the query plan, and (2) searching the space of plans for the selected cover and finding an optimal execution plan. The second step is typically addressed by a query optimizer and is not discussed here. One thing to note though that each query plan will have index scans at the leaves and posting list intersections (merge-join over sorted streams) at internal nodes. For the first step, one has to decompose the given query into a set of subtrees, each of size *mss* or less, such that the matches for each subtree can be retrieved from the index. Clearly there are multiple ways of decomposing a query and some decompositions are more amenable for query optimization. An interesting question is what makes a "good cover" from the set of all possible covers that can be obtained.

One thing we know is that the posting list size of a subtree has a direct relationship to the size of the subtree. In fact, it can be shown that the posting list size is a monotonically non-increasing function of subtree sizes for both filter-based and root-split coding. Hence, larger subtrees in a query cover are preferred since they are more selective and lead to a smaller join cost. Also for filter-based and root-split coding, one can always generate a cover of a query such that the cover includes only subtrees of maximum size *mss*, referred to as *max-cover*. However, a query can have multiple maximal covers and those covers may not all have the same cost, especially if there are overlaps between the subtrees in the covers. The number of joins is a direct function of the number of subtrees in a query cover, and having fewer subtrees will lead to fewer joins or less cost. Hence among all maximum covers, those with the least size, in terms of the number of subtrees, are preferred; such a cover is referred to as a *join-optimal cover*.

An interesting question is how one can find a join-optimal cover. Here are a few observations that can be made. First, it is clear that a join-optimal cover cannot have less than $\lceil |Q|/mss \rceil$

subtrees. Second, it is shown that it is not always possible to construct the structure of a query using a root-split cover of size $\lceil |Q|/mss \rceil$. Chubak and Rafiei [2012] give an algorithm that finds a join-optimal root-split cover of a query for $mss \leq 6$; they also bound the number of extra joins required for evaluating a root-split cover of Q by $|Q| - \lceil |Q|/mss \rceil - mss + 1$.

3.5.3   SUMMARY

Querying natural language text poses some interesting challenges in terms of storage and indexing. We presented some approaches for efficiently processing text pattern and tree pattern queries, but interesting challenges remain. In particular, for selection queries, a "good" index is expected to prune as many irrelevant sentences as possible. However, relevant sentences do not always have many overlapping terms with a query; this can make pruning a challenging task. For join queries, a "good" storage structure is expected to preserve the locality of relevant sentences, for example, storing them in the same or nearby pages. Detecting such relevance in advance of queries and balancing the access cost with the storage overhead is an interesting direction.

3.6   TRANSFORMING NATURAL LANGUAGE TEXT

Natural language text may be mapped to a formal meaning representation for further querying. The holy grail of language understanding research is finding a meaning representation that is detailed enough, allowing reasoning and inference on the transformed text, while covering as many different domains and contexts as possible. In practice, two types of meaning representations, collectively referred to as *semantic parsing* in Section 2.4, have emerged. One type of representation, referred to as *deep semantic parsing*, maps each sentence into a detailed formal model such as first-order logic predicates. A problem with deep semantic parsing is the presence of ambiguity in natural languages; a sentence can have multiple meanings, and a parser may have to decide between these meanings. This is not easy without a deep understanding of the domain or the context where the sentence is stated. Also, it is not easy to construct a general-purpose ontology that is detailed enough to be useful in all possible applications. For the same reason, deep semantic parsers have been successfully developed for specific domains (such as conversational agents [Allen et al., 1995], travel reservations, etc.) where the vocabulary is limited and an expression cannot have many possible meanings.

Shallow semantic parsing or semantic role labeling is an alternative representation where the meaning is represented using a set of smaller but somewhat independent components or analyses. These components may include named entity resolution, word sense disambiguation, and detecting the arguments of predicates or verbs of a sentence.

Irrespective of the level of semantic parsing and the degree of understanding that is reached, the output of a semantic parser is a set of n-ary predicates about a domain of discourse. The output may also link the mentions of named entities and predicates in parsed text to external resources and ontologies, for the purpose of resolving entities and disambiguating predicates. The result of parsing a document may be represented as a knowledge graph with nodes denoting entities or literals and edges depicting the predicates. Such a graph can be queried using ontology graph query languages such as SPARQL.

In this section, we discuss some of the steps and challenges in mapping natural language utterances to a formal representation.

3.6.1 MEANING REPRESENTATION

When we talk about meaning representation for natural language input utterances, there is a non-human involvement in processing and acting upon the input. The actions may vary between domains and applications but they often refer to those taken by a machine. For example, a robot may act to instructions by making a sequence of moves, whereas the actions of an emergency response system, monitoring tweets, will be detecting when and where a catastrophic event is about to hit.

As for what makes a "good" meaning representation, it must be possible to detect from the representation of a sentence the relationships that are expressed between objects and events referenced in the sentence. In a more specific setting, it must be possible to identify, based on the representation of two sentences, if both sentences describe the same relationship or event, or if the relationship described in one sentence can be inferred from the other sentence. A challenge in reaching this goal is that different sentences with possibly different word choices can express the same meaning and we ideally want all those variations to have the same canonical meaning representation.

First-Order Logic

First-Order Logic (FOL) has some attractive features for meaning representation including sound basis for expressiveness, inference and querying. FOL describe objects or the domain of discourse in terms of their properties and relationships. Each FOL formula may consist of terms (constants, variables, functions), predicates, quantifiers, and connectives (such as logical "and," "or," and "implication"). Each formula makes a statement about the universe. Here are some example formulas:

(F_1) $city(Edmonton) \land population(Edmonton, 928000) \land capital(Alberta, Edmonton),$
(F_2) $\forall c(country(c) \implies \exists p(city(p) \land capital(c, p))),$
(F_3) $city(x) \land locatedIn(x, Canada).$

FOL formulas can use constants (as in F_1) or variables (as in F_2 and F_3). Variables in a FOL formula can be free (as in F_3) when they are not in the scope of a quantifier; otherwise they are bounded (as in F_2). Formulas with free variables are useful for iterating over the elements of a domain in queries, whereas formulas with no free variables make statements about the world (referred to as first-order sentences).

The semantics of FOL is defined as a 4-tuple (U, C, P, F) where U is the universe and $C, P,$ and F are interpretations of constants, predicates, and functions, respectively. In simple terms, an interpretation associates constants, predicates, and functions in a formula to those in the real world being modeled. For example, an interpretation of F1 is to associate the constant "Edmonton" to the city of Edmonton in Alberta, "Alberta" to the province of Alberta in Canada and the numeral to an integer denoting the numeral.

Description Logics

There are often relationships between entities in the domain of interest. For example, industrialized countries, developing countries, and European countries are all countries. Description Logics (DL) have emerged as a logical formalism for ontologies (such as Web Ontology Language or OWL) and as a means for describing the relationships between entities and their domains or categories. Suppose we have identified a set of categories within our domain of interest (or state of affairs). Many of these categories may have relationships that must be specified in the meaning representation. For example, the assertion that an European country is a country or an industrialized country is a country can be expressed as a subsumption relation between the categories:

$$EuropeanCountry \sqsubseteq Country$$
$$IndustrializedCountry \sqsubseteq Country$$

The aforementioned relations between European country, industrialized country, and country are examples of Terminological (aka TBox) axioms, describing the relationships between related terms, in DL, whereas the statement "city(Edmonton)" is an assertional (aka ABox) axiom, describing the category of a named entity. Relational (aka RBox) axioms, on the other hand, state that, for example, the categories *IndustrializedCountry* and *DevelopingCountry* are disjoint, *EuropeanCountry* and *IndustrializedCountry* overlap, and the composition of *sisterOf* and *sonOf* is subsumed by *nephewOf*.

As for supporting inference, DL focuses on tasks such as if a category is a subset or a superset of another category or if an entity is a member of a category, given the facts about the entity and the categories. The reasoning system for DL goes beyond the explicitly stated facts and infers relationships that are not explicit. Unlike FOL where the definition of semantics is procedural and the reasoning is in general computationally infeasible,[6] DL includes fragments of FOL for which the tractability of inference can be guaranteed and efficient reasoning techniques are developed [Baader et al., 2008, Tsarkov and Horrocks, 2006].

Representing Events

Representing events and states is a major part of the semantics that needs to be captured in natural languages. A state can be seen as a property or condition that remains unchanged over a period of time, whereas an event is a change in states. Events generally don't have a fixed number of arguments. For example, a meeting can have two, three, or more participants and a single

---

[6]This is due to infinitely many structures that can be created in the presence of function symbols.

predicate with a fixed number of arguments cannot represent these variations. One approach for representing events is to treat them as entities and introduce an event variable that can be quantified (as shown for a meeting event):

$$\exists e \ \ meeting(e) \ \land participant(e, Davood) \land participant(e, Yunyao) \land subject(e, BookPrep).$$

Events are often associated with a time. One event can happen before, during, and after another event, and this information must be represented to support inference. Verb tenses in a sentence provide information about the events described in relationship to other events. Reichenbach [1947] introduces *speech time, event time*, and *reference time* to distinguish events described using tenses such as past and present perfect. For example, in the sentence "I had a meeting," both event time and reference time are positioned before the speech time on the time line, whereas for the sentence "I have had a meeting," the event time is before both reference time and speech time. Using the present perfect indicates that the reference time and the speech time coincide. Temporal logic has been a formal model for representing time and reasoning about events and assertions. Each statement in temporal logic is associated with a time, and the truth of a formula with respect to an interpretation (e.g., an assignment of variables in a query) is also evaluated with respect to a time.

Events may also be associated with a location. For example, the statement "gas prices went up today" can be true in one location and not true in another location. The location of an event can be given explicitly or may be implied. In our example on gas prices, the event may be associated with the location of the speaker of the utterance. The location of an event may be represented in the form of a latitude and a longitude. Events may also be associated with a location in a geographical database of locations, known as a gazetteer. The hierarchical structure of a gazetteer gives Part-Of and other relationships between locations that can be useful in performing an inference.

3.6.2   MEANING OF WORDS

Following the principle of compositionality, the meaning of a sentence may be determined in terms of the meanings of its constituents, i.e., words, and the rules governing the composition. Here a sentence is not simply treated as a bag of words and other factors such as the ordering of the words, the grouping of words into phrases and the relationships that exists between words affect the meaning of the sentence. As the syntactic composition of a sentence is governed by a grammar, the semantic composition may also be guided by the break-down of the syntactic components and their relationships, for example, represented in the parsing of the sentence. In this section, we discuss how meaning can be assigned to words.

A simple approach to representing the meaning of a word is to take each word on its face value, as a symbol with no analysis or relationship. However, the meaning of a word cannot always be defined independent of other words. Two words may be related or have the same or similar meanings. As an alternative, the meaning of words may be defined in terms of the distribution of words around it, by embedding it into a vector space. Two words that are synonyms are expected to co-occur with the same context words and have the same or similar vectors. The size of this vector can be large (in the order of the size of the vocabulary) with many zeros, and a dense embedding may be obtained, for example, using Word2vec models [Bengio et al., 2003, Mikolov et al., 2013b].

Sometimes a word can be broken down into smaller units and the meaning of the word may be defined in terms of that of its canonical form (aka lemma) and suffixes and prefixes. A word may also have more than one sense or aspect, depending on the context it is used in, and these senses of the word sometimes are semantically related (known as polysemy) and sometimes are not (referred to a homonymy). Different word senses with different canonical forms may also be related. The relationships may take the form of synonymy, for two senses that are substitutable one for the other in any sentence without changing the sentence truth, or hyponym-hypernym, when one sense is a subclass of another sense (e.g., Canada-Country). Other relationships include antonymy, part-whole, etc.

We generally need a more comprehensive account of the relationships between word senses, and this leads to resources or databases such as WordNet and FrameNet that have such information.

WordNet, created under the direction of a psychology professor at Princeton University [Miller, 1995a] starting in 1985, is one of the commonly used resources for English. The database groups word senses into nouns, verbs, adjectives, and adverbs. The latest version, wordNet 3.0 released in 2005–2006, has 117,798 nouns, 11,529 verbs, 21,479 adjectives, and 4,481 adverbs. On average, the number of senses for a noun, a verb, an adjective, and an adverb is, respectively, 1.24, 2.17, 1.40, and 1.25. For example, "database" has one sense whereas "order" has 15 senses as noun and 9 senses as verb. For each word sense, the database has a set of near-synonyms (referred to as synset). For example, one noun sense of "order" is club (as in "royal order of Canada") and this sense has the following synonyms: club, social club, society, guild, gild, lodge. A verb sense of the word is "bringing into conformity with rules" and this sense has the following words in the synset: regulate, regularize, regularize, and govern.

Events

Representing the meaning of events is not as simple as that of word senses since events have arguments and those arguments often have semantic constraints on them. In describing those constraints, two events may be deemed similar and are grouped together because of the same or similar constraints placed on their arguments. Consider the following publishing and editing events:

$$\exists p, \exists b \; publishing(p) \wedge publisher(p, \textit{"Morgan} - \textit{Claypool"}) \wedge published(p, b) \wedge book(b)$$
$$\exists e, \exists b \; editing(e) \wedge editor(e, \textit{"Jagadish"}) \wedge edited(e, b) \wedge book(b).$$

The FOL description given above is event-specific and does not provide much ammunition for inference. For example, it is not easy to see that editor and publisher have similar roles in that they make the editing and publishing events to happen. They both, referred to as an *agent*, represent someone or something that is the source of the causation or action. Book, which is affected by the action, is referred to as *theme*. Arguments may take other thematic roles such as force, result, beneficiary, goal, etc. Semantic role labeling systems assign thematic roles to arguments (instead of syntactic roles such as subject and object) since the ordering of verb arguments can change (e.g., "send him the book" and "send the book to him") and so is their syntactic role labels. However, it is generally difficult to come up with a standard set of thematic roles or even formally define each role. An alternative approach is to come up with more general semantic roles such as *agent* and *semantic role - patient*. The more an argument shows agent-like properties such as deciding on, committing to or causing a course of action, the more likely the argument is labeled a *proto-agent*. Similarly, the more an argument takes patient-like properties such as passive or stationary compared to the other participant, causally affected instead of affecting, going through some changes due to the actions contributed to the other participant, the more likely the argument is a *proto-patient*.

Resources have been developed to aid with representing meaning at the thematic role level. Two of those commonly-used resources are Propositional Bank (referred to as PropBank) and FrameNet.

PropBank [Kingsbury and Palmer, 2002] is a collection of sentences annotated with semantic roles. The English version annotates all sentences in Penn TreeBank. Each sense of each verb has a set of roles or arguments. Generally, the first and the second arguments are, respectively, proto-agent and proto-patient and the other arguments are specific to each verb. For example, the frame file for verb "expect" lists two roles: expector as Arg0 and the thing expected as Arg1, whereas the verb "leave" has more than one sense. One sense of the verb, which means "moving away from" as in "Joe left the town," has two roles: entity leaving as Arg0 and the place left as Arg1. Another sense of the verb, which means "give" as in "Joe left his friend an apartment in his will," has three roles: giver as Arg0, the thing given as Arg1, and the beneficiary as Arg2.

FrameNet [Baker et al., 1998] provides semantic role labels at the level of a frame, which describes a situation instead of a specific verb. Frames can span over multiple verbs and nouns, and the arguments of a frame are broken down into core and non-core elements. For example, the "lending" frame has three core arguments including borrower, lender and the theme (i.e., the object being transferred), and a few non-core arguments including duration, manner, place, purpose and time. The frame "expectation" has three core arguments including a cognizer (i.e., someone who believes something will take place), a phenomenon (i.e., what cognizer believes in) and a topic, and a set of non-core arguments including the degree to which the event occurs, a location, a time, etc. Another example of a frame and a sentence labeled with frame roles is given in Section 3.3.2.

3.6.3 COMPUTING WORD SEMANTICS

One subject that we haven't touched in our discussion is the issue of ambiguity in mapping to a meaning representation. Suppose we are given a sentence and our goal is to annotate each word or phrase with a semantic role label. Each word of the sentence can have multiple senses in our lexicon such as WordNet or FrameNet; which one of those senses does accurately model the sense of the word in the sentence? In a different scenario, a query word may not have a matching word in the corpus. Which other word senses in the corpus are similar to the given query word? In this section, we review some techniques for addressing these problems.

Word Sense Disambiguation

Each word in a sentence has a set of context features that may help predict its sense. Consider the word "order," which has 15 senses as noun in WordNet. Knowing the words to the left and to the right of the target word can reveal the sense of the word that is used in the sentence. For example, the words right before and right after the target word "order" in "the troop received an order to withdraw" are different than those for "the speed was an order of magnitude faster" and may reveal the sense of the word. In general, a window may be placed on the target word to extract these features. The features may include the words in the window, their positions with respect to the target word, and their part of speech tags. The context features may also include non-stop words in a larger window, as a bag of words, giving the topic of the context where the target word is used.

Several approaches have been developed to detect the sense of a word used in a sentence. One simple baseline is to always choose the most frequent sense of each word, based on the frequency of the senses in an annotated corpus. This strategy usually correspond to the first sense of the word in WordNet; for example, for the word "order," it will correspond to the sense described as "a command given by a superior." This clearly will miss many other senses of the word. Another commonly used strategy, known as the Lesk algorithm [Lesk, 1986], selects the sense of the word whose dictionary description is the closest to the context of the word being disambiguated. The closeness, in what is known as the simplified Lesk Algorithm, is measured in terms of the number of non-stop words in common between the context of the word being disambiguated and the words in the dictionary definition and examples of the sense. When the overlap is less than a threshold, meaning that there is no strong evidence in favor of choosing one sense, the algorithm selects the most frequent sense of the word.

A problem with the simplified Lesk method is that the dictionary definition of a word is often short and a correct sense may not have enough words in common with the target word context. The Corpus Lesk algorithm addresses this problem using a corpus to extend the size of the dictionary description. The idea is to extend the set of words in the dictionary definition of a sense and to include all words in the corpus sentences that are labeled for that sense. Due to a potential increase in the number of overlapping words, the Corpus Lesk method also introduces a weight to each word, instead of simply using a stop word list. The weight of a term is the standard IR Inverse Document Frequency (IDF), which is inversely proportional to the number of documents (in this particular case, the number of dictionary entries or senses) the word appears in. Supervised approaches are also employed for word sense disambiguation but are not discussed here.

Word Sense Similarity
Sometimes we want to detect if two words or word senses are similar. For example, in Recognizing Textual Entailment (RTE), two sentences are given and the RTE system must predict if one sentence can be entailed from the other despite the differences in word choices and their composition. In Question Answering (QA), the question words can be different than the words in answer sentences, and the QA system must find such sentences despite the vocabulary differences.

The algorithms for computing word similarity can be grouped into thesaurus-based and distributional. Thesaurus-based algorithms are applicable when there is a thesaurus (e.g., Word-Net) that lists the words being compared. Suppose the senses of the words are known and each sense corresponds to a node in the thesaurus. In a simple thesaurus-based algorithm, the distance between two word senses is measured in terms of the length of the shortest path between them in the thesaurus hierarchy. With this definition, a word sense is more similar to its parent and children than the word senses that are far apart. When the word senses are not known, the distance between two words w_1 and w_2 may be defined as

$$sim_{word}(w_1, w_2) = min_{\substack{s_1 \in senses(w_1) \\ s_2 \in senses(w_2)}} sim_{senses}(s_1, s_2).$$

Our simple algorithm assumes all paths of the same length are of the same distance (or the same similarity). It is not hard to verify that this does not always hold. For example, two nodes that are closer to the root of the tree are expected to have a shorter distance, compared to nodes that are placed deeper in the tree, but they may not be more similar.

Resnik [1995] defines for each concept node c the probability that a randomly selected node in a corpus is an instance of the concept c. Let $P(c)$ denote this probability. Based on this notion of probability, Resnik defines the similarity between two word senses s_1 and s_2 as $-log P(LCS(s_1, s_2))$ where LCS is the lowest or deepest node in the hierarchy that subsumes both s_1 and s_2. Lin et al. [1998] argues that a similarity function should measure not only the commonalities but also the differences between the word senses being compared. He defines the similarity between two senses s_1 and s_2 as

$$sim(s_1, s_2) = \frac{2log P(LCS(s_1, s_2))}{log P(s_1) + log P(s_2)}.$$

Note that the numerator has a constant multiplier for normalization purposes and to make sure the similarity between the same senses is 1.

Thesaurus-based algorithms are applicable only if a thesaurus is available and both words are listed in the thesaurus; this cannot be warranted for many words especially those that are domain specific. Distributional algorithms, on the other hand, estimate the similarity based on word distributions in a corpus. The idea behind distributional algorithms is that the meaning of a word can be inferred from its context in a corpus. The algorithms differ on how they represent the context and how two contexts are compared (e.g., Lin [1998a]). A simple algorithm is to take the words that occur in the neighborhood of a target word and construct a feature vector of their co-occurence frequencies, based on which the similarity can be estimated. It can be noted that a simple co-occurence frequency cannot be a good measure since many non-content words such as "a", "the," and "of" co-occur with the target words as well as with any other word. A fix is to avoid using absolute frequencies, and instead measure for each context word, its relative frequency of co-occuring with the target word compared to chance. This can be expressed for context words x and y as their pointwise mutual information, i.e.,

$$pmi(t,c) = log \frac{P(t,c)}{P(t)P(c)},$$

where the numerator gives the observed co-occurence probability of context word c with target word t and the denominator gives the probability of co-occurence assuming independence.

The Word2vec models learn a word embedding by training a neural network model that can predict the context words. On the other hand, a model that can predict the context words also gives a good embedding as far as the similarity between the words is concerned. These models are usually efficient in representing the context and are now widely used [Witten et al., 2016].

Given two words and their feature vectors, as constructed above, the word similarity can be computed using a similarity metric such as Cosine, KL-divergence, etc.

3.6.4   MEANING OF SENTENCES

To make inference at the level of a sentence and to support queries that generalize over different surface text of predicates and the ordering of arguments, we need a meaning representation at the sentence level to describe the predicates and the semantic roles of their arguments. A general approach to represent this commonality between different verbs and predicates in a sentence is to label each verb with a verb sense (as in Propbank) or a frame (as in FrameNet) and to assign thematic roles to their arguments. Table 3.5 gives some of the common thematic roles a noun phrase may take with respect to an action or event described by a verb. For example, in the sentence "John gave a lecture to students," *John* is the agent, *the lecture* is the theme, and *students* is the experiencer. The roles stay the same even if the syntactic structure of the sentence changes, for example, to "John gave students a lecture." Levin [1993] classifies English verbs into 47 high-level classes and presents multiple argument structures the verbs can take. VerbNet [Palmer, 2018] extends Levin's classes and also maps PropBank verbs to VerbNet classes. The 2006 version of this resource [Kipper et al., 2006], which is the latest as of February 2018, lists 5,257 verb senses (of 3,769 lemmas), each mapped to one of 274 classes and 23 thematic roles are used for labeling the arguments.

Table 3.5: A set of commonly used thematic roles (source: Palmer et al. [2010b]).

Role	Description	Example
Agent	Initiator of action, capable of volition	**The man** stopped the car.
Patient	Affected by action, undergoes change of state	The man broke **the window**.
Theme	Entity being moved or located	The man stopped **the car**.
Experiencer	Perceives action but not in control	**John** felt sorry for the boy.
Beneficiary	Beneficiary of the action	John rented **him** a car.
Instrument	Instrument used to carry out the action	He used **his chisel** to carve out the ears.
Location	Place of object or action	He moved to **California**.
Source	Starting point	He walked home from **his school.**
Goal	Ending point	He walked **home** from his school.

However, as noted earlier, it is difficult to come up with a standard set of thematic roles and a consistent mapping of arguments. A simpler approach is to use very few general semantic roles such as *agent* and *patient* and classify each argument based on the degree they show agent-like or patient-like properties.

With the thematic role labels fixed, the semantic role labeling of an input sentence may be carried out as follows.

1. Parse the syntactic structure of the sentence and detect the dependency and constituency relationships between words or phrases.

2. Traverse the parse and find all words (mostly verbs) that indicate a predicate.

3. Find the arguments of each predicate in Step 2 by examining the nodes in the parse tree and assigning a semantic role when applicable.

For the last step, a supervised classifier, trained on resources such as ProbBank and FrameNet, may be used. The classifier expects a feature vector for each node. Typical features include the predicate (usually a verb) since the roles are defined with respect to a predicate. They also include the POS tag of the node (e.g., NP), its dependency relationship to the predicate (e.g., Subj), the headword of the node, and the path in the parse tree from the node to the predicate. An initial list of these features is reported by Gildea and Jurafsky [2002].

Sometimes the verb of a sentence imposes restrictions on the class of entities or concepts that can fill the argument roles, and these restrictions become constraints on predicate arguments. For example, the sentence "John drinks a tea" makes sense whereas the sentence "John drinks a building" does not because we expect the theme of the verb "drink" to be something that is drinkable. One way to address this is to associate arguments to a thesaurus type or class (e.g., Wordnet synsets). In practice, such restrictions on arguments are expressed as soft constraints since violations can occur and those violations can be acceptable. Resnik [1993] captures this with *selectional preference strength* which gives the the degree at which a predicate identifies the semantic class of its arguments.

Word2vec models are extended to provide a dense vector representation of a sentence. A simple approach is to use a weighted average of the word vectors [Mikolov et al., 2013b, Mitchell and Lapata, 2010]. An alternative approach is to combine the word vectors in an order determined by the parse of the sentence [Socher et al., 2011]. Paragraph vector is another approach that assigns each paragraph a vector, which is later averaged or concatenated with the word vectors [Le and Mikolov, 2014].

3.6.5 INFORMATION EXTRACTION

Semantic role labeling is a resource-intensive process. A syntactic parser must iterate over many possible parses before coming up with a parse that is consistent or has less ambiguity; the cost of parsing increases dramatically with the length of the input. Annotated data are needed for detecting events and labeling their arguments; the accuracy of this mapping largely depends on the size and the coverage of labeled corpora, and constructing such resources is a lor-intensive process. Information Extraction (IE) has emerged as a set of techniques for extracting structured information about entities and their relationships without a full syntactic parsing and also often without the need for large and comprehensive annotated data.

One area of information extraction, referred to as *template filling*, assumes a predefined set of templates can be provided. The semantic role of arguments for those templates may be learned from a labeled corpus [Bunescu and Mooney, 2004, Chieu et al., 2003] before the learned models can be used to classify the input relations and to extract more instances or slot fillers of the templates. Several tasks are defined under template filling. For example, the Message Understanding Conference (MUC)[7] ran evaluations on the following information extraction tasks: named entity recognition, coreference resolution, template element (which extracts basic information about organization and person entities), and scenario template (which extracts event information and relating them to organization and person entities) [Chinchor, 1998, Sundheim and Grishman, 1996]. As an example, an entity element template of type person in MUC-7 includes for each person the name (e.g., "Dennis Gillespie"), the category (e.g., person_military), and the description (e.g., "Capt." | "the commander of Carrier Air Wing 11"). An example of a

---

[7]MUC refers to a series of Message Understanding Conferences, also known as MUC-1, …, MUC-7, which ran from 1987–1998. The conferences, funded by DARPA, provided evaluation benchmarks for information extraction systems.

scenario template task in MUC-4 is extracting terrorist related events, where the slots include incident date, incident location, event type (e.g., bombing, kidnapping), instrument (e.g., bomb, arson), perpetrator (i.e., person and organization names), target, etc.

Another area is *open information extraction*, which has gained interest lately with the need for extracting structured information from documents on the Web. Unlike template filling, the schema in open IE does not need to be fixed in advance. Early open IE systems extract triplets in the form of (subject, relation, object) from relations expressed by a verb; examples include TextRunner [Banko et al., 2007] and ReVerb [Etzioni et al., 2011]. Later systems attempt to extract non-binary relations and also relations that are not verb-based; this usually comes at a cost. For example, OLLIE [Fader et al., 2011] and Stanford OpenIE [Angeli et al., 2015] use dependency parse of a sentence to extract some of those relationships. For example, OpenIE extracts the open domain relation was-born-in(Obama, Hawaii) from the text "Obama was born in Hawaii," where the sentence verb becomes the relation name.

Information extraction techniques can be grouped into rule based and machine learning based. Rule-based approaches use hand-crafted and sometimes semi-automatically generated rules and regular expressions to extract the desired information. Our query-based approaches discussed in this chapter fall under rule-based approaches. The rule-based approaches are widely used in many domains and applications [Chiticariu et al., 2013]. Chieu et al. [2003] report that almost all participating systems in the scenario template task in MUC were rule-based systems. Two tutorials in SIGMOD outlined some of the challenges and opportunities in rule-based information extraction from a database perspective [Chiticariu et al., 2010, Doan et al., 2006]. Machine learning-based approaches may train a classifier for each slot in a template. The features considered may include verbs and noun phrases that are linked to the slot, for example, in a dependency parse and the roles. For example, Chieu et al. [2003] consider a range of features for each candidate noun phrase (np) including the verbs associated with the np as an agent, the verbs associated with the np as a patient, the head word of the np, etc. Any supervised learning algorithm may be used for the classification. The approaches used in the literature include maximum entropy [McCallum et al., 2000], support vector machine, naive Bayes, decision tree, and conditional random fields [Peng and McCallum, 2006].

3.6.6   ENTITY LINKING

Named entities mentioned in text can have multiple interpretations in the real world, and a transformed text will be ambiguous unless those interpretations are resolved into one. For example, consider the sentence "Paris has fallen in love with 'garden skyscrapers'." GeoNames[8] lists 97 possible interpretations for Paris as a place name. Other interpretations include person name, film title, music band, music album, etc. (for example, as listed in Wikipedia[9]). Entity linking, also known as named entity disambiguation, refers to the task of determining a correct

---

[8]http://www.geonames.org
[9]https://en.wikipedia.org/wiki/Paris_(disambiguation)

interpretation for each name from the set of candidates. The set of possible interpretations is usually taken from a knowledge base, and there are a few resources that are widely used.

Resources. The list of candidate entities for entity linking may be obtained from different sources. Wikipedia currently has over 5 million articles, each typically describing an entity or a concept. This resource provides a vast amount of disambiguation clues about a large class of prominent named entities, and is often used for entity linking [Cucerzan, 2007]. These clues include contextual words (from the body of an article describing an entity), entity surface forms (from linked pages) and category tags. GeoNames is another resource that covers a relatively large number of location names and is used for resolving named entities of type location [Kamalloo and Rafiei, 2018]. The database currently has over 10 million geographical names, with populated places identified and alternate names also given. Yago [Suchanek et al., 2007] constructs its knowledge base by combining data from Wikipedia, WordNet, and GeoNames. With over 10 million entities (such as people, organizations and locations) and more than 120 million facts about those entities, it is the largest knowledge base in public domain. Yago adopts the taxonomy of WordNet and the category system of Wikipedia and has about 100 manually defined relationships of different types between entities. These include *subClassOf* (e.g., physicst subClassOf scientist), *type* (e.g., AlbertEinstein type physicist), and *means* (e.g., "Einstein" means AlbertEinstein).

Techniques. Entity linking can be broken down into : (1) candidate generation and (2) candidate ranking. In the first phase, each entity mention in a document is assigned a set of candidates that may resolve the entity. The candidates may be obtained from a knowledge base (or other sources as discussed above), based on the string comparison between the surface form of the mention and that of the entity. Sometimes the same entity is mentioned multiple times in the document. For example, a person can be referred to as "John Doe" early in the document and as "Doe" or "John" later. These variations can provide additional clues in finding the set of candidates. For example, "Doe" may be expanded to "John Doe" before looking up the candidates. Entity linking may identify these variations in surface form and resolve them all to the same entity.

For candidate ranking, both supervised (e.g., Bunescu and Paşca [2006], Kulkarni et al. [2009], Zheng et al. [2010]) and unsupervised approaches (e.g., Cucerzan [2007], Gottipati and Jiang [2011]) are used. Generally, the candidates may be ranked based on (1) how the surface form of the mention compare to that of the candidate, (2) whether the entity types match, and (3) if the context of the mention matches that of the candidate. It is usually assumed that entities mentioned in a document are related and their resolving entities must also demonstrate some topical coherence. The popularity of the candidate entities may also be taken as the prior probability in ranking, in that popular candidates will have a better chance of correctly resolving a mention. A survey of the main approaches to entity linking is reported by Shen et al. [2015].

3.6.7   SUMMARY AND DISCUSSIONS

We reviewed semantic role labeling and some of the components that play a key role in transforming natural language sentences to a meaning representation. Our review included meaning representation frameworks (e.g., FOL), resources for computing the meaning of words and sentences (e.g., WordNet, VerbNet and FrameNet), detecting and representing event arguments, and identifying similarities between words and events. There are other important components that are not discussed including named entity detection and resolution, representing and reasoning on time and location of events, and pronoun resolution. A more detailed overview of semantic role labeling with a survey of related work is provided by Palmer et al. [2010b]. Semantic role labeling was the shared task in CoNLL 2004 and 2005, which allowed a number of systems to compete on PropBank predicate-argument structures [Carreras and Màrquez, 2005]. More recent semantic role labeling systems use deep learning models and claim to perform better. For example, a recent system claims an F1-measure of slightly over 83% on CoNLL 2005 and CoNLL 2012 test sets [He et al., 2017a].

To put our discussion into perspective, suppose we are given an article and our goal is to distill information about entities that are mentioned, their relationships, the events the entities are participating in, and the time and the location of those events. We probably want the distilled information to be organized and the temporal and the spatial relationships between events to be stored in a format that is transparent for querying. We also want the relationships between entities and events described in different articles to be correctly represented. Putting together a system that does the aforementioned tasks at a level comparable to humans is a daunting challenge and can be characterized as the ultimate goal of machine reading. However, the task may be broken down to smaller subtasks and techniques or algorithms are being developed for those subtasks on a best-effort basis.

One task is entity linking—detecting the mentions of named entities in text and resolving them to real world entities. The literature in this area assumes an independent description of the referent entities (for example, a Wikipedia page) exists [Cucerzan, 2007]. In the absence of such independent resources, the problem remains challenging. Similar challenge are faced when resolving pronouns though the techniques for resolving them are somewhat different.

Our discussion of meaning representation for a sentence leads to a set of predicates. Those predicates may describe relationships or events, each involving some entities. Such events or relationships may happen or be valid at a certain period in time. Temporal references in a sentence can be absolute (e.g., March 28, 2018) or relative (e.g., last week). Temporal references can be implicit and further analysis may be needed to place a predicate on the time axis. Despite the progress made on developing resources (e.g., the annotated TimeBank corpus [Pustejovsky et al., 2003]) and algorithms, assigning a predicate to a point or a period on the time axis can be challenging.

Events may also have spatial associations. For example, an event may happen at a location or may involve entities that have some fixed localities. Detecting and representing those spatial relationships can be important for further analysis. However, those spatial relationships may or may not be explicitly stated in text. Despite progress on toponym resolution and geo-tagging [Leidner et al., 2004, Rafiei and Rafiei, 2016], assigning general entities and events to their actual locations remains an interesting challenge.

3.7   SUMMARY

A large volume of data we consume on daily basis is stored in some form of natural language. This includes messages and comments in text and social messaging services, emails, meeting minutes, financial reports, newspaper articles, blog posts, etc. This data is too rich to be ignored and too large to be left outside databases. In this chapter, we reviewed the issues and developments surrounding storage, querying and managing natural language text data. Our discussion also included mapping natural language text to a meaning representation which has clear benefits in terms of querying and understanding text.

There have been other developments that are orthogonal to our discussion and treatment of natural language text. One such development is the issue of integrating natural language text with relational data. We are not aware of any work targeting natural language text in particular, but there is literature on integrating text and relational data, which may be applied to natural language text. This line of work can be divided into tight integration and loose integration. Chu et al. [2007] present a tight integration approach that incrementally queries the structure in text, and as more queries are processed, more structure is extracted, allowing a richer set of queries. There has been more studies on a loose integration of text and relational data where text sources are managed by a text search engine and are joined with relational data at the query time. Under a loose integration scheme, different probing strategies are studied and various cost models and query processing and optimization techniques are developed [Agichtein and Gravano, 2003, Agrawal et al., 2008, Chaudhuri et al., 1995, Jain et al., 2008]. A typical workload is entity extraction where a set of entities is stored in a relational database, and the goal is to efficiently retrieve the mentions of those entities in a set of documents [Agrawal et al., 2008]. This line of work on text can be directly applied to natural language text, though natural language text has a structure and offers more opportunities for querying and query processing, as discussed throughout the book.

Another development is on populating a relational table or a knowledge base with similar data residing in natural language text sources. The idea is to learn patterns that encode an input set of instances and use those patterns to retrieve more instances. The literature can be divided into pattern-based (e.g., Agichtein and Gravano [2000], Brin [1998]) and consistency-based reasoning (e.g., Suchanek et al. 2009). Some of the recent development in this area are reviewed by Weikum et al. [2016].

CHAPTER 4

Natural Language Interfaces to Databases

In the real world, we usually obtain information from each other by asking questions in a natural language. Not surprisingly, natural language interfaces have long been regarded as the holy grail for query interface to databases [Li et al., 2006]. Numerous science fictions include androids (e.g., Data in *Star Trek* by Paramount Pictures [1987] or Samantha in *Her* by Warner Bros. Entertainment Inc. [2013]) that allow human to retrieve data via natural language questions. An ideal natural language interface to databases enables users to pose arbitrarily complex ad hoc queries against underlying databases and obtain precise information back with minimal effort. The emerging democratization of data makes such a interface even more appealing than before [Liang, 2016], as such it requires no prior knowledge of any formal query language, database schema, or the exact terminology of the underlying data. In reality, unfortunately, despite years of research efforts [Sujatha et al., 2012], natural language interfaces to databases largely remains an open research problem.

In this chapter, we first give an overview of a typical natural language interface to databases in Section 4.1.1. We also discuss various challenges related to the building of a natural language interface to databases at the high level in Section 4.1.2. We then discuss these challenges and summarize common techniques used to address them in Sections 4.2–4.4. We will then further systematically analyze in more details a number of representative natural language interfaces to databases developed since 2000, with a focus on recent systems. This unified systematic view of the systems aim to help the readers to better understand the existing solutions and develop their owns accordingly.

4.1 OVERVIEW

In this section, we describe the main components of a modern natural language interface to databases (NLIDB). We then present the major open challenges hindering the wide adaption of NLIDBs. We will use the terminologies defined in this section throughout the rest of the chapter to help providing a systematic view of different techniques and solutions.

4.1.1 ANATOMY

Figure 4.1 depicts the anatomy of a natural language interface to databases. As can be seen, an NLIDB typically consists of the following three main components: (1) *Query Understanding*, which parses and interprets a natural language query (NLQ) into one or more intermediate representations to capture the intent of the user query; (2) *Query Translation*, which translates the intermediate representation of a user query into the corresponding structured query; and (3) *Data Store*, which executes the structured queries generated by Query Translation against the underlying data store to obtain results.

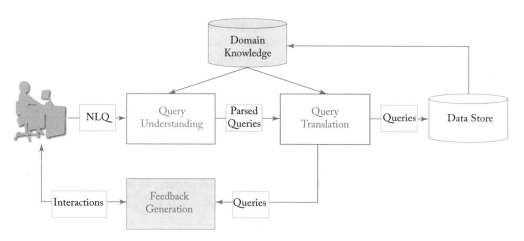

Figure 4.1: Anatomy of a natural language interface to databases.

Many modern NLIDBs also include one or two of the following components. (1) *Domain Knowledge*, which captures the domain knowledge related to the underlying data and to help with a better query understanding and translation; and (2) *Feedback Generation*, which provides feedback to the user with regards to the system's understanding and interpretation of the user query and/or solicit additional input from the user to help the system to better understand and interpret the user query.

In the rest of the chapter, we will explain these components in more details.

4.1.2 CHALLENGES

The major open challenges blocking the wide adaption of NLIDBs are related to the following two aspects: (1) *natural language understanding* and (2) *query translation*.

Natural language understanding refers to the capability of parsing a natural language query, usually in the form of one single natural language sentence, into a data structure that represents the syntactical and semantic structure of the query. Natural language understanding is the foundation of any NLIDB system.

Unfortunately, generic natural language understanding remains a challenging open research question itself [Liang, 2016]. The performance of a *parser*, the software component performing natural language understanding, is often far from ideal. Moreover, parsers used by NLIDBs are usually developed with open-domain news corpus, while the queries against NLIDBs are often domain-specific questions. As a result, parsers tend to make more mistakes when parsing natural language queries and lead to issues for the subsequent operations in NLIDBs [Popescu et al., 2003].

Query translation is the process of translating the structured representation of a parsed natural language query into the corresponding formal query against the underlying database. Even when an NLIDB fully understands a user-given natural language query, turning that structured representation into the corresponding formal query remains a challenging task. Natural language queries are usually given by a user without the knowledge of the underlying data. As such, the NLIDB needs to bridge the gap between the parsed query and the underlying data in terms of both data value as well as schema. In addition, natural languages are much more expressive than any formal query language. Therefore, generating formal queries based on a parsed natural language query is also a major challenge in building NLIDBs. As an example, given the query "*Find the most prolific authors in the DB community*" against a typical publication database, expressing the semantics of this seemingly simple natural language query in SQL would require (i) the understanding of "*most prolific*" and "*the DB community*," as well as (ii) complex operations such as *group by*, *aggregation* (e.g., *max* and *sum*), and *subqueries*.

4.1.3   SUMMARY

In this section, we describe the common components of an NLIDB and also discuss the major challenges in building an NLIDB. In the rest of chapter, we discuss various challenges related to the building of NLIDBs and summarize common techniques used to address them (Sections 4.2–4.4). We then further analyze in more details a number of representative NLIDBs developed since 2000, with a focus on recent systems. While the techniques presented in this book are not intended to be exhaustive, providing a unified systematic view of the systems should help the readers to better understand the existing solutions and develop their own accordingly.

4.2   QUERY UNDERSTANDING

Queries specified in a formal database language fully describe the query semantics based on the knowledge of the underlying database schema. Such formal queries require no further semantic interpretation and can be directly executed against the underlying database. Queries specified in natural languages, however, need to be understood and interpreted into the corresponding internal representation(s) first, before being translated into formal database queries.

Section 4.2.1 describes the scope of natural language support by NLIDBs ranging from arbitrary *ad hoc natural language queries* to strictly *controlled natural language queries* and discuss the trade-offs between the different choices.

Section 4.2.2 presents *stateless* and *stateful* designs of NLIDBs, based on whether an NLIDB takes query history into consideration.

As discussed earlier in Section 4.1.2, general natural language understanding remains an open research problem. As a result, a parser may make mistakes when parsing natural language queries. Such paring errors can propagate further and lead to mistakes made by the NLIDB. Section 4.2.3 describes different techniques in handling parser errors in recent systems and their trade-offs.

4.2.1 SCOPE

The scope of the natural language support by an NLIDB may be coarsely characterized, in terms of the types of natural language queries that it supports, into the following two categories.

Ad hoc Natural Language Queries. An ad hoc natural language query is one that cannot be predetermined in any way prior to the issuing of the query. An NLIDB supporting ad hoc natural language queries does not restrict how and what queries the user can ask in natural languages except that the semantics of the queries is expressible in the corresponding structured queries.

Controlled Natural Language Queries. Controlled natural language queries are subsets of natural language queries with restricted grammar and vocabulary.

An ideal NLIDB system should support ad hoc natural language queries and allow users to ask arbitrary natural language questions and get the correct results back, as long as the semantics of the queries can be expressed in the corresponding structured queries supported by the underlying database. Not surprisingly, a few notable NLIDBs (such as Li and Jagadish 2014 and Bais et al. 2016) aim to support ad hoc natural language queries. Unfortunately, parsing ad hoc natural language queries remains an open problem. As illustrated in Figure 4.2, while supporting ad hoc natural language queries leads to more natural user experience, it is also associated with an increase in complexity and ambiguity of user queries. The increase in complexity in user queries tends to lead to more parsing errors. NLIDBs supporting ad hoc natural language queries thus have to heavily rely on parser error handling techniques. We will discuss such techniques in Section 4.2.3 in more details. At the same time, an increase in the ambiguity of user queries makes it more challenging to automatically analyze them. To avoid misinterpret the user intent, the NLIDBs often need to solicit user input to help resolve the ambiguity. We will describe in Section 4.4 various techniques for interacting with users to resolve ambiguity in more details.

In practice, NLIDB systems often limit their scope of natural language support to a controlled subset of natural language queries with restricted grammar and vocabulary. The goal is to reduce or eliminate ambiguity and complexity and enable reliable automatic semantic analysis of the language.

For instance, PRECISE [Popescu et al., 2004] defines the notion of semantic tractability and identifies a subset of natural language queries that can be precisely translated into SQL.

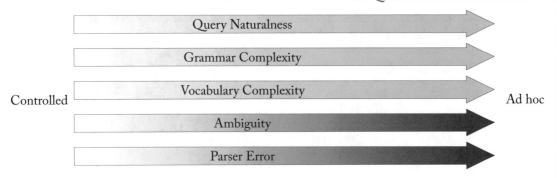

Figure 4.2: Scope of natural language support.

NaLIX [Li et al., 2006, 2007b] limits natural language queries to a controlled subset based on a predefined grammar. Similarly, NLPQC [Stratica et al., 2005] accepts queries based on a domain-specific template.

While controlled natural language queries are less ambiguous and simpler to parse, such benefits do not come for free. An NLIDB requiring controlled natural language queries needs to address two associated challenges. The first challenge is to ensure the expressiveness of the controlled language, despite of the restriction on complexity, and the usefulness of the NLIDB. Ideally, a controlled language should support as wide range of query tasks as possible. For instance, templates in NLPQC [Stratica et al., 2005] support joins between tables, and NaLIX [Li et al., 2006, 2007b] supports complex query semantics such as *aggregation* and *group by*. The second challenge is to ensure the usability of the NLIDB by helping users to understand and learn to effectively use the controlled language. One major consideration of user interaction design in an NLIDB is to expose the restrictions imposed by the controlled natural language to the users so that they can understand the limitation of the system and learn to use the controlled subset with as little frustration as possible. Section 4.4 describes various techniques in designing the user interactions in more details.

4.2.2   STATELESS VS. STATEFUL

Search is rarely a single-step process as found by previous studies [Moore, 1995, Olson et al., 1985, Peacock et al., 1992]. As such, when a user interacts with an NLIDB, she may issue more than one query. She often needs to modify her queries based on the results obtained. Furthermore, certain query semantics could be too complex to be composed comfortably into a single query sentence, and thus better expressed in a divide-and-conquer fashion.

Figure 4.3 depicts the following two kinds of design on how a user query could be handled by the NLIDB.

Stateless. The NLIDB understands and interprets each user query completely independent of any prior query issued by the user.

Stateful. The NLIDB understands and interprets each user query in the context of prior queries of the user, i.e., *query history*.

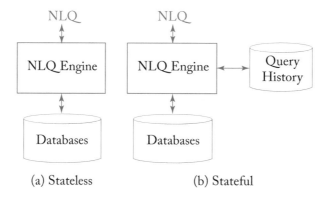

Figure 4.3: Stateless vs. stateful NLIDBs.

A stateless NLIDB does not retain query history and requires every single user query to be fully specified. Each user query is handled completely independent of each other. On the other hand, a stateful NLIDB needs to retain and use query history to understand and interpret each user query. A user query can be partially specified, and the NLIDB will interpret it based on information provided previously in the query history.

For instance, given the sample database in Figure 4.4, the user first issues a query "List all the publications by Michael Stonebraker." If the user wants to group the results by publication venues, in a stateless NLIDB, she has to issue a completely specified query such as "List all the publications by Michael Stonebraker, group by their publication venues" and repeat the information stated already in the earlier query; whereas in a stateful NLIDB, she only needs to issue a partially specified query such as "Group by publication venues," as a *follow up* query to the earlier query.

As illustrated by the above example, a stateful NLIDB interacts with users in an iterative fashion: a user asks a question, obtains an answer, and based on the answer asks follow-up questions to augment or change earlier questions. Stateful NLIDBs are also known as *conversational* NLIDBs. They can be viewed as a special type of *dialog systems* [Jurafsky and Martin, 2009b].

Compared to their stateless peers, stateful NLIDBs provide a more natural interaction environment for their users. Meanwhile, they also face a few additional challenges in query understanding. The first challenge is how to identify the relevant prior queries in the query history to help understand the current query. The second challenge is how to incorporate the relevant prior queries identified to better understand the current query. The third challenge is that users are more likely to issue partial queries and thus potentially lead to more parser errors.

Perhaps due to the additional challenges faced by stateful NLIDBs, almost all NLIDB systems developed so far are stateless with few exceptions. One notable stateful NLIDB is

Author

AuthorID	AuthorName	Affiliation
M001	Michael Stonebraker	MIT
J002	Jeffrey D. Ullman	Stanford University
H003	H. V. Jagadish	University of Michigan
…	…	…

Publication

PubID	AuthorID	Title	Year	Venue
001	M001	The design and implementation of INGRES	1976	TODS
002	J002	Introduction to Automata Theory, Languages, and Computation	2006	SIGMOD Record
004	H003	Structural joins: A primitive for efficient XML query pattern matching	2002	ICDE
…	…	…	…	…

Figure 4.4: Sample database with `Author` and `Publication` tables.

NaLIX [Li et al., 2007b]. The *iterative search* capability in NaLIX draws inspiration from "chat room"-style and forum-style interfaces. In NaLIX, queries are organized into *thread*s as in forum-style interfaces to maintain the context of each query. Meanwhile, the interaction for each individual query is synchronous as in a chat. Queries within the same thread share the same *context center*, i.e., *topic of interest*. Constraints specified in queries with regard to the context center are referred to as *query context*. The start of a thread is a *root query*, which specifies the context center and the initial query context. A follow-up query inherits and modifies the query context of its parent query and creates its own query context. NaLIX then interprets each query based on its query context and context center. If a new query specifies a new context center, then it is regarded as a new root query and starts a new thread. As a result, NaLIX allows users to incrementally focus their search on the objects of interest. More details are discussed in Section 4.5.3.

One notable recent work in enabling stateful NLIDBs appears in Suhr et al. [2018]. This work modifies the encoder-decoder architecture of recurrent neural network (RNN) [Elman, 1990] to encode context from the interaction history to make generation decisions for each natural language query (utterance). For each natural language query, the decoding step explicitly maintains a set of query fragments generated from previous queries. The decoder then chooses whether to output a token or select a segment from the set, which is appended to the output in a single decoding step maintains. Evaluation over ATIS [Hemphill et al., 1990] demonstrates the effectiveness of the proposed techniques in supporting conversational queries against databases.

4.2.3   PARSER ERROR HANDLING

NLIDBs usually leverage off-the-shelf linguistic parsers to obtain the initial syntactic and/or semantic structure of the input queries, as an initial step of query understanding. Obviously, the performance of linguistic parsers directly impact the performance of the final query. Many NLIDBs choose to make the simple assumption that the off-the-shelf parsers would always work perfectly.

Unfortunately, as discussed earlier in Section 4.1, the linguistic parsers used to parse the input queries in an NLIDB can make mistakes and produce erroneous output. The accuracy[1] of the state-of-the-art dependency parser is 92.17% over news corpus [Andor et al., 2016] and around 80% over questions [Judge et al., 2006]. As a result, while completely relying on linguistic parsers makes the design of NLIDBs simpler, users of such NLIDBs may face more frustration due to unexpected results.

There are two common approaches for handling parser errors in an NLIDB.

> **Auto-Correction.** This approach automatically detects and corrects parse errors before query translation.

> **Interactive Correction.** This alternative approach leverages user interaction and corrects parser errors in an interactive fashion.

The ideal approach toward handling parser errors is auto-correction, as it requires no effort from users. However, detecting and correcting arbitrary parser errors is not easier than building a perfect linguistic parser. As such, some of the NLIDBs (e.g., PRECISE [Popescu et al., 2003, 2004] and DaNaLIX [Li et al., 2007a]) remedy this issue by detecting and correcting certain types of parser errors.

For instance, PRECISE examines attachment decisions made by the parser. It first examines whether a noun phrase or a prepositional phrase n is attached to a parent p in an inconsistent way with the semantic information in the lexicon of PRECISE. Whenever it finds an inconsistency, it attempts to repair the parse tree by traversing the path in the parse tree from p to the root node. It searches for a suitable node to attach n to in an iterative fashion. The search stops when PRECISE finds a new node, to which when n is attached, the modified parse tree agrees with PRECISE's semantic model.

Consider, for example, the question "What are flights from Boston to Chicago on Monday?"; as depicted in Figure 4.5a, the parser wrongly attaches the prepositional phrase "on Monday" to "Chicago" instead of "flights." PRECISE is able to detect that this syntactic decision is inconsistent with the semantic information. According to its lexicon, the preposition "on" takes a flight and a day as input, instead of a city and a day. Then PRECISE attempts to re-attach "on Monday" to the ancestor nodes of "on" until it correctly attaches to the NP "flights from Boston to Chicago." Such *semantic overrides* can help PRECISE to fix prepositional attachment errors

---

[1]In term of labeled attachment score (LAS) [Kubler et al., 2009].

as well as parser errors in topicalized questions (e.g., "What are Boston to Chicago flights?") and in preposition ellipsis (e.g., when "on" is omitted in the question "What are flights from Boston to Chicago Monday?").

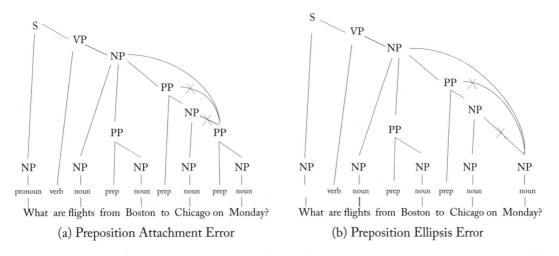

(a) Preposition Attachment Error   (b) Preposition Ellipsis Error

Figure 4.5: Example semantic override for parser error repairing in PRECISE.

Unfortunately, many parser errors are difficult to be systematically identified and automatically corrected. Such errors could be addressed via interactive corrections by soliciting user input in one of two ways. One way is query reformulation. Whenever the system detects possible parser errors but is uncertain on how to correct the error, it can report an error message and alert the user to rewrite the current query into one that can be correctly handled by the parser (e.g., NaLIX [Li et al., 2006, 2007b]). In such cases, the system can also potentially learn how to correct similar errors automatically in the future (e.g., Li et al. [2007a]). The other way is parse tree correction, where the system detects possible errors and asks the user to correct the parse tree directly so that the current query can be correctly understood by the system (e.g., NaLIR [Li and Jagadish, 2014]).

4.3 QUERY TRANSLATION

The second component of an NLIDB is *query translation*. Once a natural language query is parsed into a *structured representation*, this representation is then further interpreted and translated into a *structured query* in a formal query language (e.g., SQL/XQuery/SPARQL) against the underlying database. This step can be challenging, even when the structured representation correctly and fully captures the user intent in the original natural language query, as discussed in Section 4.1.2.

Section 4.3.1 describes different aspects of the gap between parsed natural language queries and the underlying data in databases.

Section 4.3.2 describes how NLIDBs generate structured queries that can be then executed against the underlying databases to produce query results, leveraging various techniques used by NLIDBs to bridge the gap in order to produce and disambiguate *interpretation*s of the parsed queries.

4.3.1   BRIDGING THE SEMANTIC GAP

The structured representation generated by query understanding is not sufficient on its own to produce a structured formal database query due to the gap between the user queries and the underlying data. A crucial role of query translation is to bridge this gap. This section describes the related challenges and provides an overview on techniques to address these challenges.

Vocabulary Gap

Users of an NLIDB are unlikely to have precise knowledge of the underlying data. As a result, there often exists mismatches between the vocabulary used in a user query and that in the underlying data.

As an example, when a user issues the query "List all the publications by Jeff Ullman" against the sample database in Figure 4.4, the NLIDB needs to construct the following SQL query in order to retrieve the desired results:

```
SELECT P.*
FROM Author A, Publication P
WHERE A.AuthorID = P.AuthorID
  AND A.AuthorName = 'Jeffrey D. Ullman';
```

Note that this query is not exactly a direct translation from the input natural language query: In particular, the table name in the SQL query is `Publication` instead of `publications`; similarly, the comparison predicate in the SQL query is `A.AuthorName = 'Jeffrey D. Ullman'`, a term that exists in the database, instead of `A.AuthorName = 'Jeff Ullman'`, a term that is from the original user query but does not exist in the database. In other words, in order to construct the right SQL query, the NLIDB needs to recognize the correspondence between the database table name `Publication` and the query term "publications" as well as the correspondence between "Jeffrey D. Ullman" in the database and the query term "Jeff Ullman."

Techniques used to recognize the existence of vocabulary gap and to identify the correspondence of terms in the underlying data and those in the user queries largely falls into the following categories.

Stemming/Lemmatization. The same word may be expressed in different forms due to morphological changes, such as "publication" and "publications" in the above example. In addition, there exist families of derivationally related words with similar meanings, such as "direct" and "director." *Stemming* and *lemmatization* are two common techniques to relate such words.

Stemming is usually a crude heuristic process that remove the ends of words, usually the derivational affixes, to their stems. Lemmatization usually utilizes vocabulary and morphological analysis of words to remove inflectional endings only and to return the *lemma*, also known as the base or dictionary form of a word.

The most well-known and common used algorithm for stemming English is Porter's algorithm [Porter, 1980]. There are also other stemming algorithms such as Lovins stemmer [Lovins, 1968], Paice/Husk stemmer [Paice, 1990], and Y-Stemmer [Yatsko et al., 2009]. The basic idea of an stemming algorithm (referred to as *stemmer*) is to recognize suffix and root of a word with predefined heuristics and return the root, also known as stem, by removing the suffix.

For example, Porter's algorithm[2] identifies "s" at the end of "publications" as a suffix and returns "publication" and thus helps relate a query term "publications" with the table name "Publication." Similarly, it can help relate "directed" to "director" by stemming both into "direct." However, due to the relatively simplistic nature of stemming algorithms, they may produce incorrect results. As an example, Porter's algorithm outputs "written" for "written," instead of "write," and returns "compani" for "companies," instead of "company." As a result, it fails to help relate the right words together. As another example, it stems "operation," "operator," "operative," "operational" all into "oper" and thus can potentially lead to the *ambiguity* issue discussed later in this section.

Lemmatization algorithms (referred to as *lemmatizer*) leverage full morphological analysis to accurately identify the lemma for each word. As a result, lemmatizers tend to produce more accurate results than stemmers and do not suffer from the issues mentioned above for stemmers.

While stemming and lemmaization are both well-known techniques in information retrieval, their benefits tend to be mixed in improving information retrieval performance for English [Manning et al., 2008]. However, they are crucial for NLIDBs in bridging the vocabulary gap and translating the original query into a fully-specified formal query.

Term Expansion. The same semantics can be expressed in words/phrases such as "author" and "writer" in significantly different surface forms. Additionally, there are many words/phrases with similar but not exactly the same semantics such as "article" and "publication." Furthermore, for the same real-world entity, more than one surface form could exist. For example, "IBM" and "International Business Machine

---

[2]As implemented in Natural Language Toolkit 3.2.5 (http://www.nltk.org/).

Corporation" refer to the same company, and similarly, "Bill Clinton" and "William Jefferson Clinton" refer to the same person.

Term expansion expands or replaces query terms with alternative terms. It has been studied extensively in the information retrieval literature [Bhogal et al., 2007] as a means to address the above more complex vocabulary mismatches due to the existence of similar or related words such as synonyms or near-synonyms, hyponymy, hypernymy [Fromkin and Robert, 2013], and entity variants. Many NLIDB systems borrow this idea from the information retrieval community to map different forms of user query terms into the same term in the underlying database.

One common approach toward term expansion is lexicon/ontology-based term expansion by leveraging hard-coded lexicons (e.g., Precise [Popescu et al., 2003]). Such a relatively simplistic approach can be further augmented with off-the-shelf lexical databases such as WordNet [Miller, 1995b] (e.g., NaLIX [Li et al., 2007b] and NaLIR [Li and Jagadish, 2014]), and/or domain-specific ontologies (e.g., NaLIX [Li et al., 2007b] and ATHENA [Saha et al., 2016]).

Recent NLIDBs, such as NaLIR [Li and Jagadish, 2014] and SQLizer [Yaghmazadeh et al., 2017], also leverage language embedding techniques such as word2vec [Mikolov et al., 2013a] in identifying the mapping between mismatched terms.

More sophisticated term-expansion functions can also be built using the knowledge of underlying structure in the representation of entities and map mentions of the same entity with different surface form by converting them into the same standardized form. For instance, ATHENA [Saha et al., 2016] leverages normalization functions for specific entity types such as Person and Organization in building its translation index. Such normalization functions can standardize mentions of different surface forms (e.g., "William Jefferson Clinton," "William J. Clinton," and "Bill J. Clinton") into the same mention (e.g., "Bill Clinton") and thus help to map query terms with the terms in the underlying databases. This type of functions can be manually crafted such as the ones used in ATHENA or learned from examples with tools such as LUSTRE [Qian et al., 2018].

Leaky Abstraction

Without the precise knowledge of the underlying database, users of an NLIDB often make the wrong assumption on the abstraction associated with the database, such as its data schema and domain ontology. Such mismatches between the database abstraction and user assumptions are referred to as *leaky abstraction*.

As an example, given the sample database in Figure 4.4, a user without a precise knowledge of the database schema may ask "Who has published the most in the top database conferences?" With this query, the user wrongly assumes that the database contains information on the types (e.g., *conference* vs. *journal*) and associated research areas (e.g., *database*) of different publication venues and that it includes information on the ranking of these venues and the notion of *top venues*.

One way to handle the leaky abstraction issue is to identify and ignore possible mismatches and reduce the original user query into one that can be handled by the database. For instance, the original query "Who has published the most in the top database conferences?" may be reduced into "Who has published the most?" For an NLIDB that handles leaky abstraction in this way, it is crucial for it to communicate back to the user and explain what is and what is not understood by the system to help the user better understand the capability of the NLIDB as well as gain more knowledge about the underlying database [Li and Jagadish, 2014, Li et al., 2007b].

Another way to handle leaky abstraction is to identify and alert the user for possible mismatches and request the user to reformulate. In systems like NaLIX [Li et al., 2006, 2007b], for example, when a user asks "Who has published the most in the top database conferences?", the system will provide feedback and guidance to help the user to reformulate it into one that can be handled correctly by the NLIDB, such as "Who has published the most at SIGMOD, VLDB, ICDE, and EDBT?"

NLIDBs can also leverage domain knowledge to help bridge the semantic gaps caused by leaky abstraction. Domain knowledge can be captured in different forms, such as ontology or domains-schema [Li et al., 2007b, Saha et al., 2016]. It can be hand-crafted or automatically learned from external resources or query reformulations. As an example, DaNaLIX [Li et al., 2007a], the domain-adaptive extension of NaLIX [Li et al., 2006, 2007b], can learn transformation rules that can be used to transform a parse tree that is not understandable by the system into one that is (Section 4.5.3).

Under-Specification

Formal database queries follow specific query syntax and require all the information expressed explicitly in order to correctly execute the queries. In contrast, a natural language query supported by NLIDBs, even in a controlled language setting, may not explicitly include all the information needed in the corresponding formal database query. This phenomenon of omitting information in natural language queries is referred to as the *under-specification* of natural language queries. Under-specified queries are pervasive in natural language interfaces such as NLIDBs [Sajjad et al., 2012].

As an example, for the sample database in Figure 4.4, to find all the publication by Michael Stonebraker, one can issue the following SQL query:

```
SELECT P.*
FROM   Author A, Publication P
WHERE  A.AuthorID = P.AuthorID
  AND  A.AuthorName = 'Michael Stonebraker'.
```

As can be seen, this query fully specifies all the information needed to execute the query, including the table names (i.e., Author, Publication), column names (i.e., AuthorID,

AuthorName), join predicates (i.e., `A.AuthorID = P.AuthorID`), comparison predicates (i.e., `A.AuthorName = 'Michael Stonebraker'`), and the SELECT clause.

Alternatively, the user may also issue the following natural language query: "*List all the publications by Michael Stonebraker.*" As can be seen, unlike the above SQL query, this query only partially specify the SELECT clause (i.e., "List all the publications") and a comparison predicates (i.e., "by Michael Stonebraker"). As such, in order to be able to construct the corresponding SQL query, an NLIDB needs to add all the missing information, such as table names and column names.

As partially illustrated by this example, two major factors contribute to the underspecification of a natural language query. First, users of an NLIDB typically have no precise knowledge of the underlying data or a formal query language. As such, they tend to formulate natural language queries that omit information important for constructing the formal queries but unnecessary for conveying the query semantics. For instance, table/columns names and join conditions are important in the formal queries but they are determined by the underlying database schema and thus are often omitted in natural language queries. Second, underspecification is a known phenomena occurring often in natural language expressions [Pinkal, 1996]. In fact, omitting certain information in the natural language queries has been found crucial in ensuring the naturalness of the queries perceived by the users [Kokkalis et al., 2012]. It is therefore important for an NLIDB to be able to gracefully handle under-specified queries and add the appropriate missing information back when constructing the final queries.

Techniques proposed to address the underspecification issue of natural language queries largely fall into the following categories.

Controlled language. One way to address the underspecification issue of natural language queries is via limiting the scope of natural language queries that are supported using a controlled language and minimizing the degree of underspecification. For instance, if an NLIDB enforces a controlled language with the grammar of `Select` $\langle TABLE_{NAME} \rangle$ `where` $\langle ATTRIBUTE_{NAME} \rangle$ `is` $\langle ATTRIBUTE_{VALUE} \rangle$, then the earlier under-specified query "List all the publications by Michael Stonebraker." will need to be rewritten into a fully specified query "Select publications where author is Michael Stonebraker" to be accepted by the NLIDB. As can be seen, controlled languages simplify both query understanding and query translation. Not surprisingly, many NLIDBs (e.g., Li and Jagadish 2014, Li et al. 2007b) require a controlled language despite of the known drawbacks discussed earlier in Section 4.2.

Repair Rule. Another way to address underspecification is to repair the underspecified natural language queries by automatically adding missing information. For example, NaLIX [Li et al., 2006, 2007b] leverages a pre-defined set of rules to add join predicates and determine the scope of nesting and grouping. Similarly, SQLizer [Yaghmazadeh et al., 2017] iteratively refines *program sketch* (i.e., partial SQL queries with placeholders for missing information) based on the database schema and data statistics with a deterministic algorithm.

Intermediate Query Language. Certain intermediate query languages such as Schema-Free XQuery [Li et al., 2004], Schema-Free SQL [Li et al., 2014a], and OQL [Saha et al., 2016] can accept queries that are not completely specified with respect to the underlying database schema. The corresponding engines that support these query languages can execute such queries either directly (e.g., Schema-Free XQuery [Li et al., 2004]) or by translating the queries into the corresponding formal query languages such as SQL or SPARQL (e.g., OQL [Saha et al., 2016]). Instead of translating a natural language query to a formal query language that requires fully specified information, an NLIDB can translate it into an intermediate query language that allows certain missing information and thus reduces the work required to handle the under-specification issue.

Ambiguity

The major role of query translation is to find a mapping between a natural language query q_{nl_i} and its corresponding structured query $q_{structured_i,j}$, denoted as $\langle q_{nl_i}, q_{structured_i,j} \rangle)$ and referred to as an *interpretation*. Natural language is highly ambiguous by nature [Wasow et al., 2005]. It is not unusual for an NLIDB to find that multiple interpretations of the same natural language query are possible when attempting to bridge the semantic gaps between user queries and the underlying databases using the techniques described earlier. In another word, the same natural language query may be potentially mapped into more than one structured query.

The key questions to consider when an ambiguity arises are the following.

Interpretation Ranking. When multiple interpretations are possible, arbitrarily returning results for all the interpretations can only overwhelm and confuse the user. Instead, an NLIDB needs to either select one single interpretation to produce the final results for the user or return an ordered list of results associated with the interpretations. In either cases, the interpretations need to be ranked.

To rank the interpretations, one common approach is for the NLIDB to associate each interpretation with a score, where the score corresponds to how confident the NLIDB is in generating that particular interpretation. As an example, given the query "Find all SIGMOD publications by Michael Stonebraker" against the database in Figure 4.4, an NLIDB could translate it into the following three SQL queries, since the term "SIGMOD" could be interpreted as the "SIGMOD" conference, or the "SIGMOD Record," or both.

```
(Q1) SELECT P.*
     FROM Author A, Publication P
```

```
            WHERE A.AuthorID = P.AuthorID
                AND A.AuthorName = 'Michael Stonebraker'
                AND A.venue = 'SIGMOD';

    (Q2) SELECT P.*
            FROM Author A, Publication P
            WHERE A.AuthorID = P.AuthorID
                AND A.AuthorName = 'Michael Stonebraker'
                AND A.venue = 'SIGMOD Record';

    (Q3) SELECT P.*
            FROM Author A, Publication P
            WHERE A.AuthorID = P.AuthorID
                AND A.AuthorName = 'Michael Stonebraker'
                AND (A.venue = 'SIGMOD'
                    OR
                    A.venue = 'SIGMOD Record')
```

For simplicity, assume that the NLIDB assigns a confidence score based on the average Jaccard distance [Jaccard, 1901] between the original query terms and the corresponding database terms used in the interpretation. Then we can obtain the following confidence scores:

$$s_{Q1} = J(\text{``}SIGMOD\text{,''}\text{``}SIGMOD\text{''}) = 1$$
$$s_{Q2} = J(\text{``}SIGMOD\text{,''}\text{``}SIGMODRecord\text{''}) = 0.5$$
$$s_{Q3} = \frac{J(\text{``}SIGMOD\text{,''}\text{``}SIGMOD\text{''}) + J(\text{``}SIGMOD\text{,''}\text{``}SIGMOD\text{''})}{2} = 0.75.$$

As such, we can rank the interpretations such as the corresponding queries are in the order of $Q1$, $Q3$, and $Q2$. In practice, more factors could be taken into account in assigning the confidence scores in addition to the term similarity, such as closeness in the database schema and the size of the results returned.

User Interaction. When an NLIDB discovers potential ambiguities, attempting to translate a NLQ, one important decision to make is whether to surface and how to surface the ambiguity to the end user. It can choose to hide the ambiguity from the user and make the decision automatically. Alternatively, it can also choose to surface the ambiguity to the user.

The reason to surface ambiguity is two-fold. First, it helps a user to better understand the capability of the NLIDB. No matter how well an NLIDB handles the ambiguity issues, it could make mistakes. Surfacing the ambiguity discovered by the NLIDB could help a user to better understand the semantic gaps between the knowledge in the user's mind and the underlying data as well as the system's capability in bridging the gaps. Second, it allows the NLIDB to solicit user input to help resolve the ambiguity. For instance, NaLIR [Li and Jagadish, 2014] generates a multiple choice selection panel for each ambiguous part and requires a user to resolve the ambiguity manually. ANNESAH [Shabaz et al., 2015] performs automatic disambiguation. However, it also surfaces system decisions at the point where the ambiguity matters via interactive ambiguity widgets to allow the user to resolve ambiguities. User inputs are stored as constraints and influence subsequent queries, similar to how domain knowledge is acquired in DaNALIX [Li et al., 2007a].

4.3.2 QUERY CONSTRUCTION

The construction of queries in a formal language from natural language queries can be done by constructing formal queries from parsed queries with a deterministic algorithm or via machine learning (e.g., Bais et al. 2016, Tang and Mooney 2001), resolving ambiguity and augmenting queries with additional information with techniques discussed above (e.g., Amsterdamer et al. 2015b, Saha et al. 2016) as needed. We will discuss both approaches in this section. The target query language can be a formal query language such as XQuery or SQL that can be executed directly against one single underlying data store, or a intermediate language that is independent of underlying data stores such as OQL.

Algorithmic Approach

The common approach for query construction is using a deterministic algorithm to construct formal queries from an internal representation of the original natural language query, along with domain knowledge corresponding to the underlying database(s). As illustrated in Figure 4.6, algorithmic approaches for query construction largely fall into two categories: (1) *query composition*, where a parsed query is first interpreted based on information of the underlying database and then the interpretations are mapped into query fragments, based on inference rules, before finally being assembled into complete queries; and (2) *query mapping*, where a parsed query is mapped directly into a complete query based on inference rules, and in some cases, if no complete query is created, the incomplete query, referred to as *query sketch*, is repaired in an iterative fashion until a complete query is generated.

Majority of the existing NLIDBs, such as NaLIX [Li et al., 2007b], NL$_2$CM [Amsterdamer et al., 2015b], FREyA [Damljanovic et al., 2012, 2013a], NaLIR [Li and Jagadish, 2014], and ATHANA [Saha et al., 2016] construct queries via query composition. This step-by-step process is easy to incorporate the various techniques discussed above, particularly those requiring user interactions, to help bridge the semantic gap between a user-given natural language query and the underlying database. This query mapping method makes it is easier to apply template-

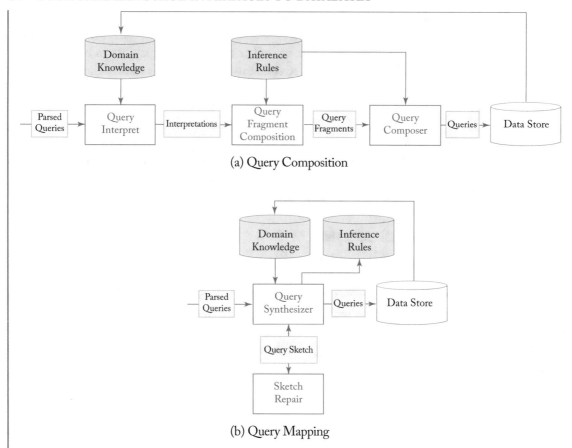

Figure 4.6: Overview of algorithm approach for query construction.

based algorithms such as in NLPQC [Stratica et al., 2005] and potentially allows more complex reasoning during the query construction process as in SQLizer [Yaghmazadeh et al., 2017].

Machine Learning Approach
A growing number of NLIDBs in recent years attempt to leverage machine learning in the construction of their structured queries beyond learning from user feedback. These efforts largely fall into the following two categories.

>   **Hybrid.** Some systems take a hybrid approach and use a combination of machine learning and deterministic algorithm approach. For instance, Palakurthi et al. [2015] presents a system that learns to map *explicit attributes* (i.e., attributes mentioned explicitly in the original natural language query) into SQL clauses and then uses the deterministic

algorithm approach to construct the full SQL queries. Meanwhile, the work described in Giordani and Moschitti [2012] uses a generative parser to generate candidate SQL clauses, composes them into complete SQL queries with rules, and then uses a SVM-ranker to rerank the candidates queries. SQLizer [Yaghmazadeh et al., 2017] takes a similar approach: It first trains a semantic parser to obtain query sketches, uses a rule-based approach to repair the sketches into complete SQL queries, ranks all the queries during the process, and finally presents the top *m* results to the user.

Purely Machine Learning. The growing popularity of sequence to sequence models has led to NLIDBs being built with machine learning models that perform the mapping from the original natural language query to the corresponding structured query without using any intermediate meaning representation. In such NLIDBs, query understanding and translation is performed together. For instance, Iyer et al. [2017] uses a neural sequence-to-sequence model to directly generate SQL queries from natural language questions and then leverages user feedback to improve the model in an iterative fashion. Another recent work Seq2SQL [Zhong et al., 2017] leverages the structure of SQL when generating SQL queries with a deep neural network with policy-based reinforcement learning to help improving the model during training. Last but not the least, Suhr et al. [2018] is an interesting recent work that leverages query history in generating SQL queries from natural language dialogs with databases.

While building an NLIDB completely with a machine learning approach may appear to simplify the overall design of the system, it also needs to address a few unique challenges.

Training Data. The quality of the machine learning models obtained heavily depends on the quality and quantity of the training data. How to scale up the building of training data remains a challenge. Not surprisingly, this challenge has received increasing attention [Brad et al., 2017, Zhong et al., 2017]. It would be interesting to adapt techniques used in building training data for general-purpose semantic parsers [Wang et al., 2015], such as crowdsourcing and paraphasing, for building NLIDBs, while taking advantage of the existing knowledge about the target language and the underlying data.

Expressivity. Formal database query languages aim to be *relationally complete* [Codd, 1972], i.e., be equivalent in expressive power to relational algebra. Existing work (e.g., Iyer et al. 2017, Yaghmazadeh et al. 2017, Zhong et al. 2017) learns only a small subset of SQL. Building machine learning models that are capable of performing complex logical reasoning remains an open challenge.

Explainablity. Due to the black-box nature of machine learning models, it is even more challenging for a user to understand the limitations of the system. Iyer et al. [2017]

make a preliminary attempt in this direction, but enabling a better explainablity remains an open problem for machine learning in general.

Overall the work on applying machine learning approaches for constructing NLIDBs is still at its early stage. Many dimensions are yet to explored. However, with the fresh wave of ambition pushing the limits of what can be machine learnable, it is an exiting time to study how to incorporate machine learning in building better NLIDBs.

4.4 USER INTERACTIONS

As depicted in Figure 4.1, user interactions is an integral part of an NLIDB. In this section, we discuss various aspects related to user interactions in an NLIDB. We first describe different design considerations when building an NLIDB (Section 4.4.1). We then present several user interaction models applicable to an NLIDB (Section 4.4.2). Finally, we discuss how the choice of stateless vs. stateful impacts the user interactions of an NLIDB.

4.4.1 DESIGN CONSIDERATIONS

When designing user interactions for an NLIDB, it is important to take the following into consideration.

Learnability. How long does it take for users to learn to use the NLIDB competently? This consideration is especially important for NLIDBs supporting controlled languages (Section 4.2.1), as any query out of the scope will result in errors (e.g., Li and Jagadish 2014) or will produce a less desired result (e.g., Saha et al. 2016).

Explainability. Given a result returned by an NLIDB, can a user understand why the result is obtained? This consideration is crucial for a user to understand the capability of an NLIDB.

System Response Time. Once a user submits a natural language question, how long does it take for the system to translate it into a formal query and how long does it take to execute the query and return a result? It is important to understand the user expectations and constraints on system response time and design the user interactions accordingly (e.g., providing clear UI indication when something is in progress).

4.4.2 USER INTERACTION MODELS

We introduce a few commonly used user interaction models in NLIDBs, summarized as follows.

Result Explanation. An NLIDB needs to make many choices to return a result based on an input NLQ. In addition to returning the result itself, an NLIDB may also allow a user to trace back and understand all the choices made by the NLIDB (potentially with the help from the user).

Interpretation/Query Navigation. As discussed in Section 4.3.1, due to the semantic gap between a user-given NLQ and the underlying database, an NLIDB may translate the same NLQ into one or more formal queries. An NLIDB would pick the top-ranked query, execute it and return the results to the user [Saha et al., 2016]. NLIDBs using the *Interpretation/Query Navigation*, however, present all or the top-*k* of the interpretations/queries and allow the user to navigate them to pick one that is intended (e.g., Li and Jagadish 2014). To support this interaction model, an NLIDB needs to present the choices in a way that is easily consumable for its users (e.g., presenting formal queries along with its English descriptions) to help the user understand the choices and reduce their mental burden.

Conversational Clarification. Given the ubiquitous nature of ambiguities in NLQs, successfully resolving ambiguities is crucial when building an NLIDB. An NLIDB can explicitly solicit user input to help resolve the ambiguities via UI prompt (e.g., pop-up with a list of choices or with auto-generated questions).

Failure Clarification. An NLIDB may fail to translate an input NLQ. In such a case, it is important to explain to the user the cause of the failure and possible ways of reissuing a new input NLQ (e.g., Li et al. 2007b).

Query History Navigation. When an NLIDB preserves query history, even partially (e.g., Li et al. 2007b), it also needs to allow the user to view and navigate in the query history, so the user does not need to reissue an old query.

It is worth noting that the above user interaction models are also useful when designing a programming-by-example system, where the system has to bridge the gap between the example and a intended program. For instance, the concepts of *Program Navigation* and *Conversational Clarification* in Mayer et al. [2015] are similar to the concepts of Interpretation/Query Navigation and Conversational Clarification discussed above.

4.4.3 STATELESS VS. STATEFUL

As discussed in Section 4.2.2, depending on whether an NLIDB is designed to remember preceding natural language queries or user interactions, it can be categorized into stateful or stateless. In a stateless NLIDB, incorporating the user interaction models discussed in Section 4.4.2 requires only consideration of the current input NLQ. In contrast, while in a stateful NLIDB, supporting these models also requires the consideration of relevant query history and thus introduces additional complexity to the design.

4.5   NOTABLE SYSTEMS

In this section, we describe a few notable NLIDBs since year 2000 in chronicle order.[3] From Section 4.5.1 to Section 4.5.9, we provide an overview of the individual systems as well as highlight their key technical contributions. In Section 4.5.10, we summarize and compare the different design considerations of the different systems when putting together the complete end-to-end system.

4.5.1   PRECISE

PRECISE Popescu et al. [2003, 2004] is an early modern natural language interface for relational databases. It supports controlled natural language based on the notion of *semantic tractability*, defined as follows.

Definition 4.1   Database Element.   Any instance of database relations, attributes, or values is referred to as a *database element*.

Definition 4.2   Token.   A *token* refers to a word matches a database element. Depending on the type of the matching database element, a token can be further classified into a *relation*, *attribute*, or *value* token.

Definition 4.3   Syntactic Marker.   A *syntactic marker* is a term from a fixed set of database-independent terms that make no semantic contribution to the interpretation of the NLQ.

Definition 4.4   Semantically Tractable.   Given a set of database element E, a sentence S is considered *semantic tractable*, when its complete tokenization satisfies the following conditions:

- every token matches a unique data element in E;
- every attribute token attaches to a unique value token; and
- every relation token attaches to either an attribute token or a value token.

Figure 4.7 depicts the overall architecture of PRECISE. The query understanding stage leverages Charniak parser [Charniak, 2000] to obtain attachment relationship between tokens, followed by semantic override to correct certain types of parser errors such as preposition attachment and ellipsis. Details of semantic override are described earlier in Section 4.2.3 and thus omitted here. During query translation, the parse tree nodes are first mapped into different types of tokens and/or syntactic markers based on pre-built lexicon. Consider the following simple database consisting of one single table.

[3]We refer the readers to Sujatha et al. [2012] for discussions on additional early NLIDBs.

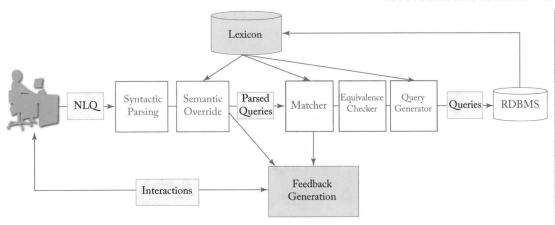

Figure 4.7: Overview of PRECISE.

Figure 4.8 depicts the corresponding tokenization post parsing for query "What the HP jobs on a Unix System." Each parse tree node regarded as tokens is then mapped into corresponding database element(s). The same parse tree node could be mapped into more than one data elements. For instance, "HP" could be mapped into both as attribute Platform as well as attribute Company. Such ambiguities are addressed using a maxflow algorithm, as illustrated in Figure 4.9. The final interpretation corresponds to the following SQL query:

```
SELECT DISTINCT Job.Description
FROM   Job, City
WHERE  Job.Platform = 'Unix'
  AND  Job.Company = 'HP'.
```

However, even with a maxflow algorithm, multiple interpretations may still exist for the same query. For instance, given the query "What are the systems analyst jobs in Austin?", the substring "system analyst" could be interpreted as jobTitle = ''system analyst'' or as description = ''systems'' and jobTitle = ''analyst.'' In such a case, the system will ask user to select one of the interpretations to help resolve the ambiguity.

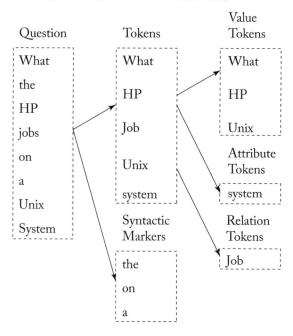

Figure 4.8: Query translation: Parse tree node mapping.

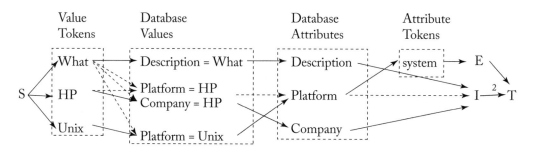

Figure 4.9: Query translation: Maxflow algorithm.

Similarly, multiple join-paths could also result in multiple valid interpretations. As an example, given the query "What are the HP jobs on Unix in a small town?" for the database shown in Figure 4.10, there are two valid join-paths from Job.JobID to City.CityID:

```
Job.JobID × WorkLocation.JobID × City.CityID

Job.JobID × PostLocation.JobID × City.CityID.
```

As a result, the system will request user input to help select from interpretations corresponding to the following two possible SQL queries:

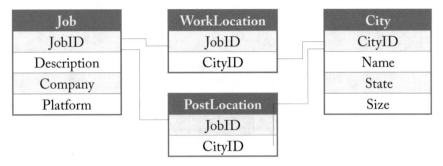

Figure 4.10: Sample job database.

```
SELECT DISTINCT Job.Description
FROM Job, WorkLocation, City
WHERE Job.Platform = 'HP'
  AND Job.Company = 'Unix'
  AND Job.JobID = WorkLocation.JobID
  AND WorkLocation.CityID = City.CityID
```

and

```
SELECT DISTINCT Job.Description
FROM Job, PostLocation, City
WHERE Job.Platform = 'HP'
  AND Job.Company = 'Unix'
  AND Job.JobID = WorkLocation.JobID
  AND PostLocation.CityID = City.CityID.
```

Main Results
PRECISE is evaluated on the ATIS dataset [Price, 1990]. The authors find that parser errors contribute to the majority of the errors and that reducing parser errors through retraining the parser and semantic override can significant improve the overall performance of the system.

4.5.2   NLPQC

NLPQC [Stratica et al., 2005] is another early NLIDB. It supports controlled NLQ based on a set of predefined rule templates. Figure 4.11 illustrates the overall architecture of the system. NKPOC uses Link parser [Sleator and Temperly, 1993] to parse input natural language questions and then map parse tree nodes into table names and attributes using some mapping rules. Then based on the table names and attributes the original question mapped into, NLPQC selects the corresponding query template to generate the final SQL query.

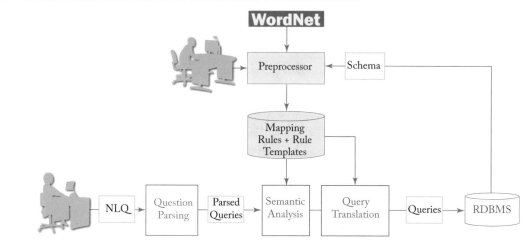

Figure 4.11: **NLPQC** overview.

The mapping rules are automatically generated using WordNet, based on the underlying database schema, and then curated by a system administrator. For instance, given a database table attribute name `language`, the system generates a mapping rule based on all terms that it may mapped into according to synonyms (e.g., *speech*, *lyric*, *words*), hypernyms (e.g., *text*) and hyponyms (e.g., *alliteration*) in WordNet [Miller, 1995b]. A system administrator then goes through the generated mapping rule to accept, reject, and/or add terms. This process could potentially generate the following mapping rule: `language` ⇒ `language, speech, words, source language`.

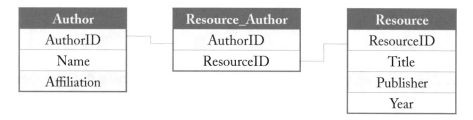

Figure 4.12: **NLPQC**: Sample database.

The rule templates are manually created by the system administrator in the form of simple action rules with if-then statements for query construction. Consider query "Who is the author of book *Algorithms*" issued against the sample database in Figure 4.11. Assume that based on mapping rules, the parse tree node "author" is mapped into table `Author`, "book" is mapped into table `Resource` and "Algorithms" is mapped into the default attribute of table `Resource`, namely `Resource.title`. Then given the following rule template:

```
If (table Author and table Resource are used)
then (related table Resource_Author is used too)
   and
    (SQL query template includes
            Resource_Author.ResourceID = Resource.ResourceID
            AND Resource_Author.AuthorID = Author.AuthorID),
```

the original query can be translated into:

```
SELECT Author.Name
FROM   Author, Resource, Resource_Author
WHERE  Resource.Title = 'Algorithm'
  AND  Resource_Author.ResourceID = Resource.ResourceID
  AND  Resource_Author.AuthorID = Author.AuthorID.
```

Main Results

Compared to other systems described in this section, NLPQC is relatively simplistic: it supports only basic SQL constructs such as selection predicates and equality joins; it does not handle parser errors or resolve ambiguity explicitly either. However, the idea of using controlled language and query templates has been widely used in practical NLIDBs systems due to the simplicity of this approach.

4.5.3   NALIX

NaLIX [Li et al., 2006, 2007a,b] is an early natural language interface for XML databases. It supports controlled natural language based on pre-defined grammar and translates natural language queries into Schema-free XQuery [Li et al., 2004], an extension to the standard XQuery language to allow under-specific queries that do not perfectly match the underlying database schema.

Figure 4.13 shows the overall architecture of NaliX. It first uses Minipar [Lin, 1998b], an off-the-shelf dependency parser, to obtain the dependency parse tree of an input natural language query. It then classifies parse tree nodes into two different types according to the following definitions.

Definition 4.5   Token.   A word/phrase that can be mapped into a XQuery component is referred to as a *token*.

Definition 4.6   Marker.   A word/phrase that cannot be mapped into a XQuery component is referred to as a *marker*.

Tokens can be further divided into different types according to the type of query components that they match based on a predefined classification tables. Similarly, markers can be

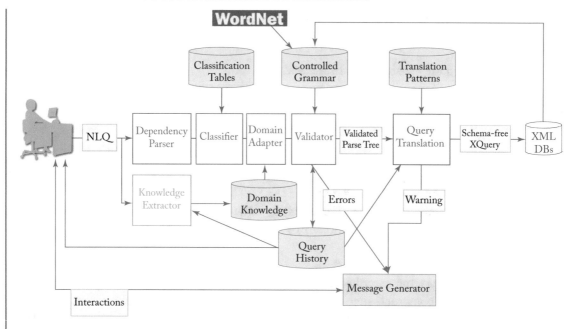

Figure 4.13: **NaLIX** overview.

categorized into different types as well. Tables 4.1 and 4.2 present example types of tokens and markers. We refer readers to Li et al. [2007b] for complete lists. Figure 4.14 illustrates the *classified parse tree* generated for query "What are the state that share a watershed with California" with different types of tokens and markers.

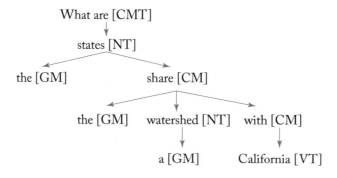

Figure 4.14: Classified parse tree.

NaLIX [Li et al., 2007a] also includes a *domain-adaptation* component that is capable of (1) extracting domain knowledge based on semantically equivalent queries and (2) incorporating domain knowledge over a classified parse tree and update it accordingly. Domain knowledge is

Table 4.1: Example token types

Token Type	Query Component	Description	Examples
Command Token (CMT)	Return Clause	Top main verb or wh-phrase [Quirk et al., 1985] of parse tree, from an enum set of words/phrases	*return* *what is*
Value Token (VT)	Value	A noun or noun phrase in quotation marks, a proper noun or noun phrase, or a number	*California* *2014*
Name Token (NT)	Basic Variables	A noun or noun phrase that is not a value token	*state* *river*
Operator Token	Operator	A phrase fron an enum set of preposition phrases	*more than* *same as*

Table 4.2: Example markers types

Marker Type	Semantics	Description	Examples
Connection Marker (CM)	Connect two related tokens	A preposition from an enum set, or nontoken main verb	*of, shared*
Modified Marker (MM)	Distinquish two name tokens	An adjective as determiner or a numeral as predeterminer or postdeterminer	*many* *popular*
Gernal Marker (GM)	None	Auxiliary verbs, articles	*a, an, the*

represented as a set of *transformation rules*, each corresponding to the mapping between a partial parse tree containing terms with domain meanings and one expressed in terms understandable by NaLIX without any domain adaption. Figure 4.15 shows the visualization of an example transformation rule applicable for the classified parse tree in Figure 4.14, resulting in the updated classified parse tree in Figure 4.16.

Before query translation, NaLIX first performs *query validation query validation*and examines the classified parse tree, potentially after incorporating applicable transformation rules, to find out whether it satisfies a predefined grammar (see Li et al. 2007b for more details). If it does, it is referred as a *valid* parse tree; otherwise, a *invalid* parse tree. An invalid parse tree will be rejected by the system with the appropriate error message(s) dynamically generated to guide the user to rephrase the query into one that is understandable by the system.

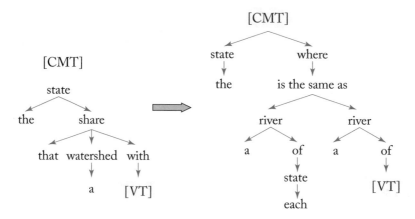

Figure 4.15: Sample transformation rule.

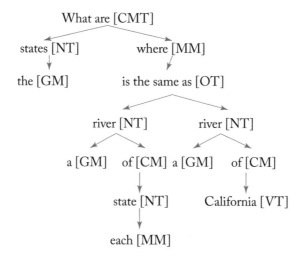

Figure 4.16: Updated classified parse tree with domain knowledge.

During the query validation process, NaLIX also performs the following two tasks whenever applicable.

Term Expansion. As described in Section 4.3.1, a user may not be familiar with the specific element or attribute names or value in the database. This task is to find the name(s) of element or attribute or value in the database that matches with a given name/value token based on WordNet [Miller, 1995b] and domain-specific ontology similar to [Li et al., 2004].

Attaching Implicit Name Tokens. A natural language query may contain one or more value tokens that have no name tokens attached to them. This task is to identify such value tokens, determine the implicit name token attached to each of them by looking up the given value in the database, and attach the implicit name tokens to the corresponding name tokens.

If multiple choices for the above task are possible, the disjunction of them (e.g., "state|province" as a name token) is used to update the classified parse tree. Users can update the query by choosing one or more of them.

Figure 4.17 illustrates the classified parse tree post query validation for our running example query, updated with (1) term expansion, where the original term "California" from the user-given query is replaced by "CA" the corresponding actual value in the database; and (2) implicit name token, where a new name token node "state" is inserted before value token "CA". Figure 4.17 also depicts *variable binding* for name tokens in the classified parse tree. As can be seen, different name tokens are associated with different variables unless they are regarded as equivalent (e.g., v_1).

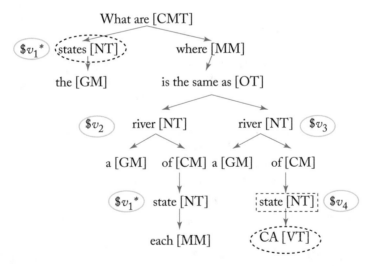

Figure 4.17: Updated classified parse tree post validation with variable binding: Dashed box indicates implicit name tokens, dashed oval indicates updated tokens via term expansion, symbol * indicates core token.

Once variable binding is done, NaLIX maps token patterns into XQuery fragments based on pre-defined patterns, including determining the scope of grouping and nesting whenever applicable. For example, our running example in Figure 4.17 corresponds to the following XQuery fragments:

```
for $v₁ in doc(''geo.xmml'')//state
for $v₂ in doc(''geo.xmml'')//river
for $v₃ in doc(''geo.xmml'')//river
for $v₄ in doc(''geo.xmml'')//state
where $v₂ = $v₃
where $v₄ = ''CA'' .
```

In addition, NaLIX maps variables corresponding to *related name tokens* into the same **mqf** function in a WHERE clause. The relatedness of name tokens is determined based on their relationship in the classified parse tree. The most common cases of related name tokens are name tokens with parent-child relationships (ignoring any intervening markers and FT/OT nodes with a single child). As an example, the parse tree in Figure 4.17 can be mapping into the following XQuery fragments:

```
where mqf($v₁, $v₂)
where mqf($v₃, $v₄).
```

We refer the readers to the original NaliX paper by Li et al. [2007b] for additional cases of related named tokens.

Finally, NaLIX constructs a complete query with all the XQuery fragments generated so far, starting from innermost clauses and work outwards. As a example, the fully translated XQuery for our running query is as follows:

```
for $v₁ in doc(''geo.xmml'')//state
    $v₂ in doc(''geo.xmml'')//river
    $v₃ in doc(''geo.xmml'')//river
    $v₄ in doc(''geo.xmml'')//state
where $v₂ = $v₃
    and $v₄ = ''CA''
    and mqf($v₁,$v₂)
    and mqf($v₃,$v₄).
```

An important functionality of NaLIX is enabling conversational-style natural language queries by supporting follow-up queries, as discussed earlier in Section 4.2.2. Inspired by "chat room" style communications and forum-style communication, NaLIX supports *iterative search* by allowing follow-up queries. Queries are organized into *thread*s as in forum-style commu-nication to maintain the context of each query, while the interaction for each individual query is synchronous as in a chat. Queries within the same thread share the same *context center*, i.e., *topic of interest*. Constraints specified in the queries with regard to the context center are referred to as *query context*. The start of a thread is a *root query*, which specifies the context center and initial query context. A *follow-up query* inherits and modifies the query context of its parent query to create its own query context. NaLIX interprets each query based on its query context and context center. If a new query specifies a new context center, then it is regarded as a new root query and starts a new thread. For instance, in our running example query "What are the states that share a watershed with California?", the context center is "the state" and the query context is "that share a watershed with California." A possible follow-up query could be "What about with Texas?." Note that this follow-up query by itself is not complete, however, by taking existing query context in the same thread into consideration, it is in effect interpreted as "What are the states that share a watershed with Texas?" However, if a user issues a new query "What is the longest river in California?," it would be considered as a new query, as the context center has been shifted to "river."

NaLIX handles query ambiguity in two ways: (1) it solicits user input for ambiguity in query terms (e.g., whether to interpret "Georgia" as a country or a state); and (2) it leverages Schema-free XQuery to find out the optimal join-path to resolve ambiguity in join-path (e.g., there could be multiple ways for a river to be related to a state). It does not do not handle parser error explicitly but has included an interactive UI to encourage NLQ input understandable by the system. It also keeps recent search history and also allows users to back up at any time, and return to any point of recent search history.

Main Results

NaLIX seeks to address almost all the challenges related to supporting natural language queries discussed earlier in this Section. It demonstrates that by leveraging a schema-free query language as a target language and carefully designed user interactions, it can support novice users to construct complex database queries (e.g., aggregation and nesting) in natural language with virtually no training. It also shows that the capability of learning-on-the-job and awareness of query search history are important for the usability of an NLIDB. It is one of the handful existing NLIDBs that supports conversational style NLQs.

4.5.4 FREYA

FREyA [Damljanovic et al., 2012, 2013a,b] is a relatively recent natural language interface designed to query ontologies. Figure 4.18 depicts its overall architecture.

One interesting aspect of FREyA is that it employs a combination of *ontology-based lookup* and *syntactic parsing and analysis* for query understanding. Ontology-based lookup links query terms to *Ontology Concepts (OCs)* with only simple morphological analysis [Damljanovic et al., 2008] without considering any context or grammar used in the given query. It uses *rdfs:label* property (by default) *rdfs:label* or any applicable predefined naming conventions to name the specific Ontology Concepts (e.g., Figure 4.19a). In addition, FREyA uses an off-the-shelf syntactic parser followed by an algorithm with heuristic mapping rules to determine *Potential On-*

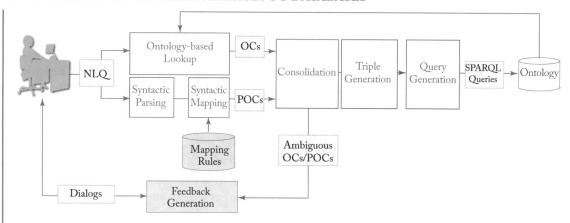

Figure 4.18: FREyA overview.

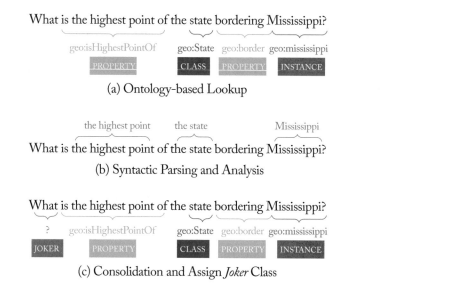

Figure 4.19: Example query understanding process in FREyA.

tology Concepts (POCs) based on a parse tree and part-of-speech tags (e.g., Figure 4.19b). The algorithm requires no perfect perfect parse tree. As such, query understanding in FREyA is relatively robust and can handle ill-form questions and query fragments.

Once FREyA identifies OCs and POCs, it seeks to map existing POCs to OCs automatically based on span containment during the *Consolidation* step. For our example in Figure 4.19, every POC in Figure 4.19b can be mapped into a unique OC in Figure 4.19a; thus no further action is required from the user. However, if FREyA fails to map a POC to an OC, it will generate a list of suggestions and ask for user feedback. The suggestions are ranked based on string similarity using a combination of Monge Elkan distance [Monge and Elkan, 1997] and Soundex [The National Archives, 2018]. For instance, POC *population* in Figure 4.20 cannot be automatically mapped into any OC. As a result, FREyaA may suggest the following OC for the user to choose from:

```
state population
state population density
has low point
...
```

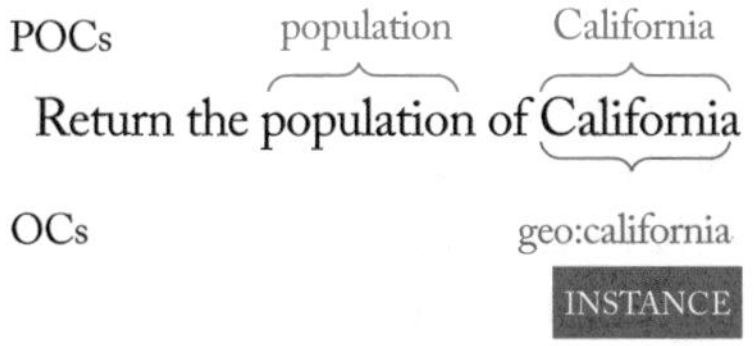

Figure 4.20: POCs and OCs mapping disambiguation.

In addition, FREyA leverages re-enforcement learning to learn to improve the ranking of suggestions based on user interactions.

Once consolidation along with any required user interaction is done, FREyA inserts *joker* based on pre-define set of rules before generating triples based on related OCs. The triples are then translated into a SPARQL query in a straightforward fashion. For our example in Figure 4.19c, a joker class is added before the first two OCs derived from the question, as they refer to a *property* and a *class*, respectively. They are then transformed into triples as follows:

```
? - geo:isHighestPointOf - geo:State;
geo:State - geo:borders - geo:mississippi (geo:State);
```

They can be translated into the following SPARQL query:

```
prefix rdf: <http://www.w3.org/1999/02/22-rdf-syntax-ns#>
prefix geo: <http://www.mooney.net/geo#>
select ?firstJoker ?p0 ?c1 ?p2 ?i3
where { { ?firstJoker ?p0 ?c1 .
filter (?p0=geo:isHighestPointOf) . }
?c1 rdf:type geo:State .
?c1 ?p2 ?i3 .
filter (?p2=geo:borders) .
?i3 rdf:type geo:State .
filter (?i3=geo:mississippi) . }
```

The result of a SPARQL query is a graph. Depending on the answer type, FREyA displays the result in different ways based on several heuristic rules. We refer the readers to Damljanovic et al. [2012] for more details.

Main Results

FREyA supports querying ontologies using natural languages. It leverages a combination of syntactic parsing with ontology-based look-up to interpret user questions and involve users to resolve ambiguities as needed. Similar to NaLIX (Section 4.5.3), it also learns from user input and self-improves overtime. It generates basic SPARQL queries with filter predicates.

4.5.5   NALIR

NaLIR [Li and Jagadish, 2014] is a more recent NLIDB designed for relational databases. As depicted in Figure 4.21, it first uses an off-the-shelf parser to obtain dependency parse tree for a given user query. Then it maps parse tree nodes into different types of nodes (Table 4.3) corresponding to SQL components they map into, in a similar fashion as NaLIX (Section 4.5.3). Specifically, the mappings are identified based on Wu-Palmer similarity score [Wu and Palmer, 1994] using surface strings and WordNet based on the database schema and value as well as predefined sets of phrases. If any node fails to map to SQL component, the system returns a warning to the user and alerts her of the failure. If a node has multiple mappings, the system selects the best mapping but reports all the candidate mappings to the user via the *Interactive Communicator*. Taking the parse tree in Figure 4.22a as an example, one possible mapping strategy is the following:

```
return → SN: SELECT
author → NN: author
more → ON: >
paper → VN: author.name
VLDB → VN: conference.name
after → ON: >
2000 → VN: publication:year.
```

NaLIR accepts controlled natural language queries based on a predefined grammar. When it cannot interpret a query based on the parse tree post node mapping, it attempts to automatically adjust the original parse tree structure into one that it can interpret, referred to as a *valid parse tree*. This step of parse tree reformulation is done based on a combination of the predefined grammar, the similarity between the reformulated parse tree and the original parse tree, and the mappings between the parse tree nodes and the schema elements in the databases. As illustrated by Figures 4.22b and 4.22c, this step is potentially useful to overcome parse errors, the

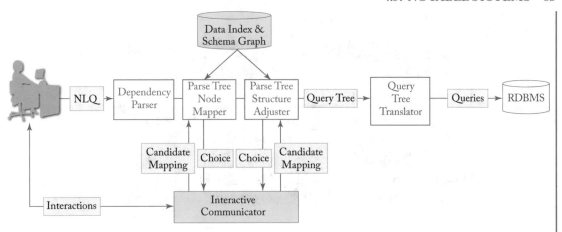

Figure 4.21: **NaLIR** overview.

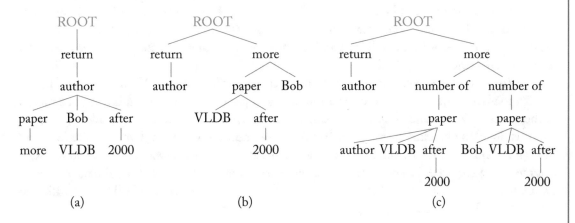

Figure 4.22: (a) A simplified parse tree; (b) a valid parse tree; and (c) a query tree after inserting implicit nodes.

limitations of semantic coverage of the system as well as ambiguity of the original query. Then the system further rewrites each valid parse tree into one semantically reasonable by inserting implicit nodes based a set of heuristic rules and generates a *query tree* (e.g., Figure 4.22c).

The user supervises this entire process. In addition, when multiple choices are available, it explicitly requests user input to resolve ambiguous mappings and interpretations. Although there is no theoretical guarantee with regard to the effectiveness of the parse tree adjustment, experimental results do seem to confirm its effectiveness.

When a query tree contains no function node or quantifier node, the translation from the query tree to the target SQL query is straightforward: each *value node* (NV) along with its

Table 4.3: Different types of parse tree node

Node Type	Corresponding SQL Component
Select Node (SN)	SQL Keyword: SELECT
Operator Node (ON)	An operator, e.g. =, >=, !=, contains
Function Node (FN)	An aggregation function, e.g., AVG
Name Node (NN)	A relation name or attribute name
Value Node (VN)	An attribute value
Quantifier Node (QN)	ALL, ANY, EACH
Logic Node (LN)	AND, OR, NOT

operation node (ON) if specified is translated to either into a SELECT clause or translated into a selection condition in the WHERE clause. Finally, *foreign-key-primary-key* (FK-PK) join paths are added based on the schema graph to connect each NV node and its neighbors, with each translated into FK-PK join conditions and all the schema elements in the join paths are added to the FROM clause.

When the query tree contains function nodes or quantifier nodes, NaLIR use the concept of *block* to identify the scope of the corresponding subqueries, where a block is a subtree rooted at the select node, a name node that is marked as "all" or "any," or a function node. The translation is done one block at a time, starting from the innnermost block. For each single block, the translation is similar to the basic translation described earlier, except that additional SQL fragments are required for connecting subqueries based on their scopes. Take the query tree in Figure 4.22c as an example. It contains three blocks and corresponds to a SQL query with two subqueries as illustrated in Figure 4.23.

Main Results

NaLIR seeks to address the challenges in query understanding and translation via a combination auto-correction and interactively soliciting user input. It demonstrates that by exposing decisions made by the system to the user and involving the user proactively in the process can effectively overcome some of the changes and provides better usability. It enables even novice users to construct complex database queries such as those with aggregation and nesting in natural language.

4.5.6   NL₂CM

Crowd mining platforms (e.g., Marcus and Parameswaran 2015) are a new emerging kind of hybrid data platform that combines knowledge bases of general data with mining the crowd for individual, unrecorded data. NL₂CM [Amsterdamer et al., 2015a,b,c] is a natural language

```
1. Block 1: SELECT SUM(Publication.name) as totalPublication
2.          FROM Publication, Conference, Author
3.          WHERE Publication.cid = Conference.cid
4.             AND Publication.id = Author.pid
5.             AND Conference.name = "VLDB"
6.             AND Author.name = "Bob"
7.          GROUP BY Conference.cid

8. Block 2: SELECT SUM(Publication.name) as totalPublication, Author.name as
   author
9.          FROM Publication, Conference, Author
10.         WHERE Publication.cid = Conference.cid
11.            AND Publication.id = Author.pid
12.            AND Conference.name = "VLDB"
13.         GROUP BY Author.id

14. Block 3: SELECT block2.author
15.             FROM (CONTENT OF 1) as block1
16.                AND (CONTENT OF BLOCK2) as block2
17.                WHERE block1.totalPublication < block2.totalPublication
```

Figure 4.23: Translated SQL query for the query tree in Figure 4.22c.

interface to crowd mining which translates natural language questions into well-formed crowd mining query in OASSIS-QL [Amsterdamer et al., 2014].

OASSIS-QL is defined as an extension of SPARQL. An OASSIS-QL query typically consists of three parts: (i) a SELECT clause, which defines the output of the query; (ii) a WHERE clause, which specifies predicates to be evaluated against a general knowledge base; and (iii) a SATISFYING clause, which defines the data pattern to be mined from the crowd. Figure 4.24 illustrates an example OASSIS-QL query, translated from the query "What are the most interesting places near Forest Hotel, Buffalo that we should visit?".

As illustrated by Figure 4.25, given such a natural language query, NL_2CM first verifies whether it belongs certain types of questions not supported by the system. For instance, "Why ..." questions are not supported. It returns warning messages to the user for such questions and provides feedback with explanation and tips for rephrasing.

If the question passes the verification steps, it is sent to Stanford Parser [de Marneffe et al., 2006] to obtain the dependency parse tree corresponding to each question along with the part-of-speech tags. The parse tree is then sent for query translation: (i) to *Individual eXpression (IX) Detector* which identifies and extracts the individual parts from the dependency parse tree; and (ii) to a *General Query Generator* for RDF data such as the FREyA system described earlier in Section 4.5.4 to process the remaining parts.

The IX Detector identifies individual parts using pre-defined IX patterns and vocabularies. NL_2CMconsiders three types of patterns/vocabularies.

```
1. SELECT VARIABLES
2. WHERE
3.     {$x instanceOf Place.
4.      $x near Forest_Hotel,_Buffalo,_NY}
5. SATISFYING
6.     {$x hasLabel "interesting"}
7.     ORDER BY DESC(SUPPORT)
8.     LIMIT 5
9.     AND
10.    { [ ] visit $x}
11.    WITH SUPPORT THRESHOLD = 0.1
```

Figure 4.24: Example OASSIS-QL query. Translated from the query "What are the most interesting places near Forest Hotel, Buffalo that we should visit?".

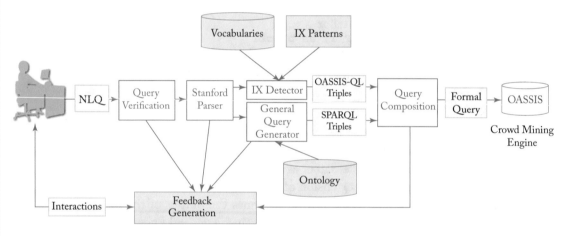

Figure 4.25: NL$_2$CMOverview.

Lexical individuality. Individual terms convey sentiment or subjectivitiy, such as "interesting," which expresses an individual opion.

Participant individuality. Participants or agents in the text that that are relative to the person addressed by the request. As an example, "you" in "Which hotel in Boston would you recommend for families with young children?."

Synctatic individuality. Certain syntactic constructs in a sentence. For instance, the modal verb "should" in "Where should we visit San Jose?" emphasizes the speaker's an opinion or sentiment about something.

Consider the natural language query in Figure 4.24, it matches a lexical individuality term "interesting" as well as the following participant individuality pattern.

```
$x subject $y
filter(POS($x) = "verb" && $b in V_participant).
```

These matches are then translated into two OASSIS-QL triples:

```
$x interesting
[] visit $x.
```

Meanwhile, the same query is also sent to a *General Query Generator* (e.g., FREyA in Section 4.5.4) to process and translate into SPARQL triples, potentially with help from the user. The ones not overlapping with detected IXs are used for further processing. For our running example, the following two SPARQL triples are produced:

```
$x instanceOf Place
$x near Forest Hotel,_Buffalo,_NY.
```

Note that the original user query only mentions "Buffalo," which refers to multiple locations (e.g., Buffalo, NY, U.S. and Buffalo, IL, U.S., etc.). In such a case, as discussed earlier, FREyA requests the user to select from a list of possible locations and produces the triple based on the user response.

Finally, the Query Composer combines the OASSIS-QL triples with the SPARQL triples into one single OASSIS-QL query. This process includes creating the sub-clauses for the SATISFYING clause (from the OASSIS-QL triples), aligning variables in the WHERE clause (from SPARQL triples), and creating the SELECT clause. For the subclauses in the SATISFYING clause, NL$_2$CM also adds support threshold or a top/bottom-k support selection based on the system configuration. The system interacts with the user to determine the final variables to be projected out by the query. Finally, the user can edits the translated query directly before starting mining from the crowd.

Main Results

NL$_2$CM takes a hybrid approach toward supporting natural language queries for crowd mining by leveraging an existing NLIDB to handle the general part of the queries. It heavily relies on user interactions to help to handle ambiguities when interpreting and translating the user queries. Experimental results obtained from experimental study, including a user study, indicate that this approach is effective for handling a wide range of user questions.

4.5.7 ATHANA

ATHANA [Saha et al., 2016] is an ontology-driven system for natural language querying of relational databases. As depicted in Figure 4.26, it takes a unique two-stage approach, where the input NLQ is first translated into *Ontology Query Language (OQL)*, an intermediate query language over an ontology, and then translated into SQL against the underlying relational databases.

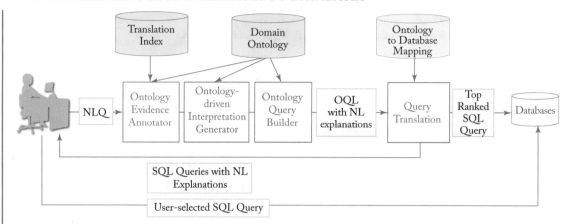

Figure 4.26: ATHANA overview.

The notion of *ontology* is defined as follows.

Definition 4.7 Ontology. An *ontology* $O = (C, R, P)$ contains a set of concepts $C = \{c_n, 1 \le n \le N\}$, a set of relations $R = \{r_k, 1 \le k \le K\}$, and a set of properties $P = \{p_m, 1 \le m \le M\}$ that represent a real-world domain.

A *ontology element* refers to a concept, relation, or relation of the ontology. It is worthy noting that an ontology based on the above definition contains no data instance, as illustrated by the example ontology in Figure 4.27. As such it is closer to an RDF Schema[4] than to an OWL ontology.[5]

OQL is an intermediate language over domain ontologies. It is designed to separate query semantics from the underlying physical data stores and support common OLAP-style queries. Figure 4.30 summarizes the portion of OQL grammar (partially[6]) supported by ATHANA.

The first stage of ATHANA, referred to as *the NLQ Engine*, consists of three components.

>**Ontology Evidence Annotator.** Given a NLQ, this components produces evidences on what are the possible ontology elements referred to by the input NLQ. Each *evidence* maps a sequence of words (referred to a *token* in this work) in the original NLQ into one or more ontology elements (concept, relation, property), referred to as *candidates*. Figure 4.29 shows all the candidates obtained for an example NLQ.

>Specifically, ontology Evidence Annotator mainly consists of two types of annotators: (i) *Metadata Evidence Annotator* uses a dictionary that maps the synonyms of

[4]https://www.w3.org/TR/rdf-schema
[5]https://www.w3.org/OWL
[6]Only single level nesting is supported.

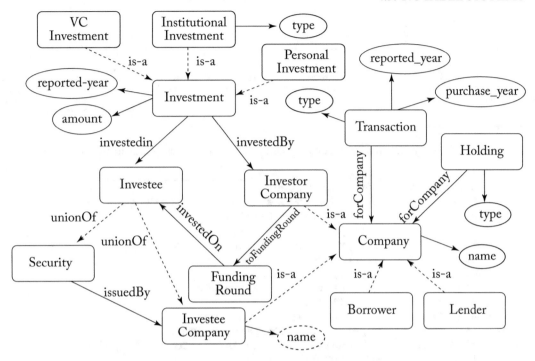

Figure 4.27: Example ontology for the financial domain.

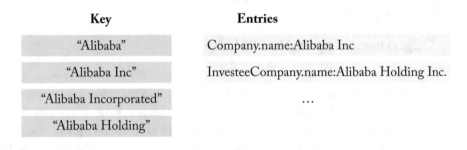

Figure 4.28: Translation index: A simple example.

the ontology elements to the corresponding ontology elements. (ii) *Data Value Evidence Annotator* uses a combination of *Translation Index*, *Time Range Expression*, and *Numeric Expression*.

Translation Index [Li et al., 2014b] is a technique adapted by ATHANA from semantic search. It provides mappings between each unique data value in the database

Figure 4.29: A NLQ annotated with evidences by the ontology evidence annotator.

```
UnionQuery:   Query (UNION Query)*
Query:        select from where? groupBy? orderBy? having?
select:       aggrType?(PropertyRef))+
from:         (Concept ConceptAlias)+
where:        binExpr1* binExpr2 inExpr?
GroupBy:      (PropertyRef)+
orderBy:      (aggrType?(PropertyRef))+
having:       aggrType(PropertyRef) binOp value
value:        Literal+ | Query
aggrType:     SUM| COUNT| AVG | MIN | MAX
binExpr1:     PropertyRef binOp [any] value
binExpr2:     ConceptAlias RelationRef+ = ConceptAlias
inExpr:       PropertyRef IN Query
binOp:        > | < | >= | <= | =
PropertyRef:  ConceptAlias.Property
RelationRef:  Relation ->
```

Figure 4.30: OQL grammar supported by ATHANA.

and its variants to one or more properties containing that value. Given a query term, it returns the set of the properties along with the actual value corresponding to the query term in the database for each property. As an example, given the term "*Alibaba*," the translation index in Figure 4.28 returns "Company.name:*Alibaba Inc*" and "InvesteeCompany.name:*Alibaba Holding Inc*," etc. The set of evidences obtained with the Metadata Evidence Annotator and Data Value Evidence Annotator is referred to as an *Evident Set V*. Each evidence $v_i : t_i \mapsto E_i \in V$ has a type (*metadata* or *data value*) and maps a token t_i to a set of candidates E_i.

In addition, the Ontology Evidence Annotator annotates dependencies between tokens in the NLQ, such as in Figure 4.29, the dependency between "*investment*" and "*Alibaba*" through "*in*," referred to as *Relationship Constraints*, formally defined later.

ATHANA does not explicitly limit the scope of NLQs it supports. Instead, if any word in the input NLQ, other than those of certain pre-defined types (e.g., prepositions, adverbs, conjunctions), fails to be mapped into any ontology element, ATHANA stops the interpretation process and returns an error message to the user.

Ontology-driven Interpretation Generator. This component takes the set of evidences produced earlier and the ontology as input and generates a ranked list of *interpretations*. Each interpretation consist of a *selected set (SS)* and a set of *interpretation trees (ITree)*, formally defined as follows.

Definition 4.8 Selected Set. Given an Evident Set V, a *Selected Set* $SS = \{(t_i \mapsto e_i) | \forall (t_i \mapsto E_i) \in V, \exists e_i \in E_i\}$. An ontology element e_i is called a *chosen element*) for evidence $(t_i \mapsto E_i) \in V$, short as a chosen element.

Definition 4.9 Interpretation Tree. Given an ontology $O = (C, R, P)$ and a selected set SS, an interpretation tree $ITRee = (C', R', P')$ and $C' \subseteq C$, $R' \subseteq R$, and $P' \subseteq P$.

Each interpretation tree $ITree$ must satisfy the constraints specified by the input query and the domain ontology. Specifically it needs to satisfy the following constraints.

Evidence Cover. It must contain the chosen element in the corresponding Selected Set. In other words, the ITree covers all the annotated tokens in the NLQ.

Weak Connectedness. The *undirected graph* created by removing the direction of the relation edges in the $ITree$ must be connected.

Inheritance Constraints. A chosen element cannot inherit a property or a relation from another chosen element who corresponds to its child (or member) concept. For instance, if a chosen element corresponds to the *Investment* concept in the ontology in Figure 4.27, then it cannot inherit the property "*type*" from its child concept *InstitutionalInvestiment*.

Relationship Constraint. A *Relationship Constraint* is a triple of tokens $\langle t_1, t_2, t_3 \rangle$ whose corresponding chosen elements e_1, e_2, e_3 in SS satisfy the following constraints: $e_1, e_3 \in C \cup P$ and $e_2 \in R$. The $ITree$ satisfies the Relationship Constraint if and only if e_2 is on the path between e_1 and e_3 in $ITree$.

Figure 4.31 shows a top ranked interpretation consisting of two interpretation trees for the NLQ in Figure 4.29. Details on how to generate and ranked the interpretation trees using a modified Steiner Tree algorithm are described in Saha et al. [2016].

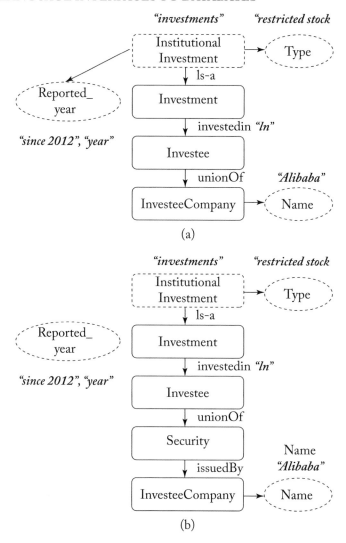

Figure 4.31: Interpretation trees in a top ranked interpretation for the NLQ in Figure 4.29.

Ontology Query Builder. This component constructs an OQL query for each interpretation by generating an OQL query that is a union of the OQL query for one interpretation tree in the interpretation.

For each interpretation tree and its corresponding selected set (SS), ATHANA generates the OQL clauses select, from, where, groupBy, and OrderBy clauses based on a combination of lexicon/pattern matches and deterministic mapping algorithms in Saha et al. [2016]. Figure 4.32 presents the OQL query generated for the Interpretation Tree in Figure 4.31a.

```
SELECT     Sum(oInstituionalINvestment.amount),
           oInstitutionalInvestment.reported_year
FROM       InstitutionalInvestment OInstitutionalInvestment,
           InvesteeCompany oInvesteeCompany
WHERE      oInstitutionalInvestment.type = "restricted_stock",
           oInstitutionalInvestment.reported_year >= '2012'
           oInstitutionalInvestment.reported_year >= Inf,
           oInvesteeCompany.name =
                              'Alibaba Holdings Ltd.', 'Alibaba Inc.',
                              'Alibaba Capital Partners'},
           oInstitionalInvestment → isa → InvestedIn → unionOf_Security
           → issuedBy=oInvesteeCompany
GROUP BY   oInstituionalInvestment.reported_year
```

Figure 4.32: An example OQL query.

> It is worth noting that when an interpretation contains more than one interpretation trees (e.g., Figure 4.31), it usually indicates the existence of ambiguity. ATHANA chooses not to explicitly disambiguate in such cases, and instead returns results for a union of them.

The second stage of ATHANA is *Query Translation*, which is responsible for converting an OQL query over an ontology into a SQL query over a database. Given an OQL query, its associated ontology, and a pre-defined *Ontology-to-Database Mapping*, the translation from OQL to SQL is done with a deterministic algorithm in a fairly straightforward manner. For the same OQL query, Query Translator generates one SQL query for each relational schema. As such, conceptually, the same NLQ query can be executed against more than one relational database at the same time.

When multiple interpretation are available for the same NLQ, multiple SQL queries will be generated. ATHANA automatically picks the top-ranked one for execution and presents the results to the user. Meanwhile, it also presents to the user a complete list of ranked SQL queries along with their natural language explanation [Luk and Kloster, 1986] to allow the user to choose an alternative query, if the top-ranked one fails to capture her intent.

Main results

ATHANA takes a ontology-driven two-stage approach in supporting natural languages against relational databases. By separating query interpretation from the actual physical store, it potentially helps to reduce the challenges associated with query understanding and translation as a user tends to be more familiar with the domain ontology than with the underlying physical database schema. In addition, this approach allows the system to generate queries on different relational schema and potentially non-relational data stores as well. Experimental results over three benchmark datasets demonstrate the effectiveness and efficiency of this approach.

4.5.8   SQLIZER

SQLizer [Yaghmazadeh et al., 2017] uses a hybrid approach to build NLIDBs with a combination of machine learning and rules. As depicted in Figure 4.33, it is constructed in two phrases—*training phase*, during which it learns a semantic parser model, and *deployment phrase*, during which it takes a NLQ as input, applies the semantic parser model learned to generate a *query sketch*, completes it using rules, and iteratively refines and repairs any low-confident query sketch using rules and heuristics until the score of the generated SQL query cannot be improved. We next explain in detail how this hybrid approach works in constructing SQL queries from natural language.

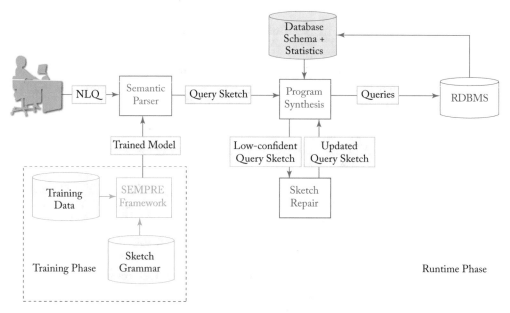

Figure 4.33: SQLizer overview.

Training Phrase

During the training phrase, SQLizer builds its semantic parser on top of the SEMPRE framework [Berant and Liang, 2014], a toolkit for building semantic parsers, as well as leverages Stanford Parser [Manning et al., 2014]. The logical form representation produced by the semantic parser are called *query sketches*, a special type of *program sketches* [Solar-Lezama et al., 2006], defined by a *sketch grammar* designed to express *extended relational algebra*.

Table 4.4: Grammar of extended relational algebra. t, c denote table and column names; f denotes an aggregate function, and v denotes a data value.

T	:=	$\Pi_L(T)\|\sigma_\phi\,(T)\|T_c\bowtie_c T \mid t$
L	:=	$L,\ L\|c\|f(c)\|g(f(c),\ c)$
E	:=	$T\|c\|v$
ϕ	:=	$\phi\ lop\ \phi\|\neg\phi\|c\ op\ E$
op	:=	$\leq\| <\ \|=\| >\ \|\geq$
lop	:=	$\vee\|\wedge$

As depicted in Figure 4.4, this grammar extends relational algebra with aggregate functions and a group-by operator (a subset of extended relational algebra supported by SQL). Specifically, aggregate functions $f \in AggrFunc = \{max, min, avg, sum, count\}$ are specified as a subscript in the projection operation. $\Pi_{f(c)}(T)$ denotes the aggregate value obtained by applying f to column c of relation T. Similarly, $\Pi_{g(f(c_1),c_2)}$ represent a group-by operation that divides rows of T into groups g_i based on the values stored in column c_2 and for each g_i, returns the aggregate value $f(c_1)$.

A query sketch χ is essentially a relational algebra term with missing table and column names, where $?h$ represents an unknown column with natural language hint h (i.e., a natural language description of the unknown), and $??h$ represents an unknown table name with corresponding hint h. The natural language hits will be used later for to help complete the query sketch. If there is no hint associated with a hole, SQLizer simply writes ? for columns and ?? for tables.

Given a set of training data consisting of pairs of English sentences and their corresponding query sketches, SQLizer learns a semantic parser that can map a given English sentence into a list of logical form x_i, each associated with a probability that the English sentence corresponds to x_i, computed using the features inherited from SEMPRE framework.

Runtime Phase

At runtime, given an NLQ, SQLizer first deploys the learned semantic parser to generates the top k most-likely query sketches, ranked by a score indicating the likelihood that the corresponding query sketch is the intended interpretation of the input query.

For instance, given the query "What is the number of papers published in SIGMOD 2015?", the highest-ranked query sketch returned by the semantic parser is $\Pi_{count(?[papers])}$ $(\sigma_{?=SIGMOD\ 2015}\ (??[papers]))$, which corresponds to the following partially specific SQL statements:

```
SELECT count(?[papers])
FROM ??[papers]
WHERE ? = 'SIGMOD 2015'.
```

In this partial SQL statement, ?? represents a unknown table, and ? represents a unknown columns, with words in the square brackets represent so-called "hints" for them. For instance, `??[papers]` indicates that the table represented by ?? semantically corresponds to the English word "*papers*."

Given a query sketch, the *Program Synthesis* component of SQLizer (Figure 4.33) enumerates through the database schema to obtain all possible well-typed *sketch completion*s by filling in as many of the holes as possible. Each sketch complete corresponds to a (potentially partially specified) SQL query. It applies a set of heuristic rules to obtain the confidence score for each sketch completion based on the following high-level intuitions; we skip the detailed algorithm in this book.

Names of schema elements. Each hole in a query sketch contains natural language hint. Sketch completion for that hole with table/column names in the database schema that is similar to the natural language hint have a higher chance to be the intended table/column.

Foreign and primary keys. Foreign keys provide links between data in two different database tables. As such, join operations involving foreign keys are more likely to be the intended term.

Database contents. The confidence score should also take the content of the database into account. For example, if there exists no entry in table T satisfies predicate ϕ, then a sketch completion corresponding to the candidate term $\sigma_\phi(T)$ should be assigned with a lower confidence score.

The above step generates a ranked list of possible well-typed sketch completions, each associated with a confidence score. In some cases, SQLizer may fail to find high-confidence sketch completion due to the existence of significant semantic gap between a user query and the underlying database, as earlier in Section 4.3.1. In such a case, the *Sketch Repair* component in SQLizer (Figure 4.33) seeks to repair the query sketch using a set of heuristic rules.

For instance, given the sample database in Figure 4.4, SQLizer fails to generate a high-confident sketch completion for the example sketch $\Pi_{count(?[papers])}(\sigma_{?=SIGMOD\ 2015}(??[papers]))$ discussed earlier, as there exists no database entry "SIGMOD 2015" in the database. In such a case, SQLizer first tries to repair the sketch by splitting the predicate $\sigma_{?=SIGMOD\ 2015}$ into two and produces $\Pi_{count(?[papers])}(\sigma_{(?=SIGMOD)\wedge(?=2015)}(??[papers]))$, corresponding to the following partial SQL statements:

```
SELECT count(?[papers])
FROM ??[papers]
```

```
WHERE ? = 'SIGMOD'
    AND ? = '2015'.
```

For the sample database in Figure 4.4, SQLizer is able to find a high-confidence completion of the updated query sketch, corresponding to the following query:

```
SELECT count(Publication.PubID)
FROM Publication
WHERE Publication.Venue = 'SIGMOD'
    AND Publication.Year = '2015'.
```

However, when we apply SQLizer over another publication database with a slightly different schema (Figure 4.34), SQLizer fails to find a high-confidence completion of this updated
sketch either, as there is no single database table contains both the entry "SIGMOD" and the entry "2015." In such a case, SQLizer tries to repair it by introducing an additional join and rewrite
the original query sketch into the following: $\Pi_{count(?[papers])}(\sigma_{(?=SIGMOD)\wedge(?=2015)}(??_?[papers] \bowtie$
$??_?))$, corresponding to

```
SELECT count(?[papers])
FROM ??[papers] JOIN ??
    ON ? = ?
WHERE ? = 'SIGMOD'
    AND ? = '2015'.
```

This time SQLizer is able to find a high-confidence completion of the updated query
sketch, corresponding to the following query:

```
SELECT count(Publication.PubID)
FROM Publication J
JOIN Venue ON Publication.VenueID = Venue.VenueID
WHERE Venue.name = 'SIGMOD'
    AND Publication.year = 2015.
```

Main Results

Takes a hybrid approach toward supporting NLIDBs by combining machine-learning and rule-
based approaches. It leverages a generic semantic parser framework to learn a semantic parser
from training data (in a database-agnostic fashion) to parse a natural language query into a
ranked list of query sketches. It then applies heuristics and domain knowledge to complete
the query sketches and repair them in an iterative fashion until it produces at least one high-
confidence well-formed SQL query. The experimental results demonstrates that Sqlizer significantly outperforms NaLIR (Section 4.5.5). The evaluation also confirms the importance of the
heuristic rules that leverage domain knowledge for sketch completion and for sketch repair.

Author

AuthorID	AuthorName	Affiliation
M001	Michael Stonebraker	MIT
J002	Jeffrey D. Ullman	Stanford University
H003	H. V. Jagadish	University of Michigan
…	…	…

Publication

PubID	AuthorID	Title	VenueID	Year
001	M001	The design and implementation of INGRES	V001	1976
002	J002	Introduction to Automata Theory, Languages, and Computation	V002	2006
004	H003	Structural joins: A primitive for efficient XML query pattern matching	V003	2002
…	…	…	…	

Venue

VenueID	Venue	Type	Publisher
V001	MIT	Journal	ACM
V002	SIGMOD Record	Journal	ACM
V004	ICDE	Conference	IEEE
…	…	…	…

Figure 4.34: Sample publication database.

4.5.9   SEQ2SQL

Seq2SQL [Zhong et al., 2017] is an NLIDB developed using deep neural network for translating natural language questions to the corresponding SQL queries. As can be seen in Figure 4.35, it is built in two phases: training and runtime. We now describe each of the phases in more details.

Training Phase

During the training phase, Seq2SQL learns a model that takes a question and a table schema[7] as input and outputs a corresponding SQL query. Figure 4.36 depicts an example table and one labeled data instance associated with the table, consisting of a natural language question,

---

[7]A table schema is the names of the columns in a table.

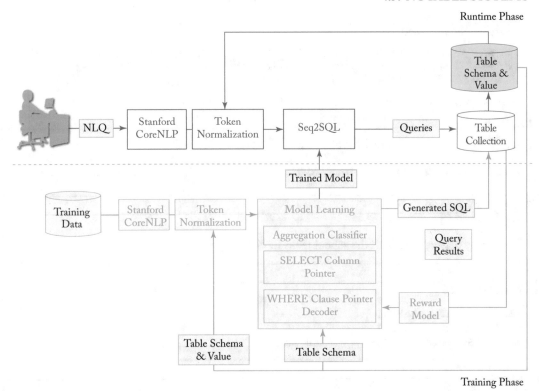

Figure 4.35: Seq2SQL overview.

its corresponding SQL query, and the result obtained from the table with the SQL query. Internally, the *Model Learning* component learns an augmented pointer network [Vinyals et al., 2015] that consists of three parts, each corresponding to a part in the most common structure in SQL queries (Figure 4.37): *Aggregation Classifier*, *SELECT Column Pointer* and *WHERE Clause Pointer Decoder*.[8] We present each of the models at high-level and skip the details on the learning algorithms in this book.

Aggregation Classifier. This classifier classifies an aggregation operation for the query, including COUNT, MIN, MAX, and the no-aggregation operation NULL. It is learned with using cross entropy via multi-layer perceptron. The cross entropy loss for the aggregation operation is denoted as L_{agg}.

SELECT Column Pointer. The selection of column(s) depends both on the table schema and the question itself. For instance, in the example query in Figure 4.36, "how many players" indicates that the query is asking for "players," which corresponds

---

[8]Seq2SQL supports only SQL queries against one table at a time, thus there is no need to learn FROM clauses.

Table: TorontoRoster

Player	No.	Nationality	Position	Years in Toronto	School Team
Mark Baker	3	United States	Guard	1998–1999	Ohio State
Marcus Banks	3	United States	Guard	2009–2010	UNLV
...	...	...	...	...	...
Rasual Butler	9	United States	Guard-Forward	2011–2012	Las Salle
...	...	...	...	...	...

Question

How many players were with the school team La Salle?

SQL Query

```
SELECT COUNT (PLAYER)
FROM [Toronto Roster]
WHERE [School/Club Team] = "Las Salle"
```

Result

1

Figure 4.36: An example table and a labeled data instance in WikiSQL dataset (simplified for presentation).

```
SELECT  $ArgFunction $ColumnName
FROM    $TableName
WHERE   ($ColumnName $op $Value)*
```

Figure 4.37: SQL structure supported by Seq2SQL. $ArgFunction \in \{$COUNT, MIN, MAX, NULL$\}$ and $op \in \{=, <, >\}$.

to the "Player" column. SELECT column prediction is therefore a matching problem, solvable using a pointer: given the table schema representations and a question representation, select a column that best matches the question. It is also learned cross entropy via multi-layer perception, where the cross entropy loss is denoted as L_{sel}.

WHERE Clause Pointer Decoder. In SQL, the predicates in a WHERE clause can be in reordered arbitrarily and still produces the same result. Learning supervised using cross entropy loss would wrongly penalize the difference in the order of predicates between a generated WHERE clause and the ground truth. As such, the model for WHERE clause is trained using policy gradient reinforcement learning. As shown in Figure 4.35, the reward is calculated by comparing the result obtained using a generated SQL against the expected result. The loss, L_{whe}, is the negative expected reward over possible WHERE clauses.

The final model of Seq2SQL is learned using gradient descent to minimize the *Mixed Objective Function* $L = L^{agg} + L^{sel} + L^{whe}$.

Last but not the least, before Model Learning, Seq2SQL applies Stanford CoreNLP Manning et al. [2014] to tokenize the natural language questions and then apply *Token Normalization* to normalize the tokens into ones that exist in the table. The exact details are not discussed in Zhong et al. [2017], but as discussed earlier in Section 4.3.1, this step is essential in bridging the semantic gap between a user query and the underlying database.

Runtime Phase

As illustrated in Figure 4.35, the runtime phase of Seq2SQL is quite simple compared to other NLIDBs discussed in this book. The core component is the *Seq2SQL* model, which takes a tokenized and normalized natural language question and a table schema as input and outputs a SQL query again the corresponding table.

Main Results

Seq2SQL showcases a machine model based on augmented pointer network that takes the common structure of SQL queries and the unordered nature of predicates into account. It demonstrates the potential of learning machine learning models that can translate NLQ into a formal database language directly without any intermediate representation. It also creates WikiSQL, a dataset of 87726 manually annotated questions and SQL query pairs over 26375 tables from Wikipedia. This large data set, despite of its simplicity (e.g., limited complexity of the queries and tables), is an important first-step to enable more efforts toward the building of NLIDBs with deep learning techniques (e.g.SQLNet proposed by Xu et al. 2017).

4.5.10 SUMMARY

Table 4.5 summarizes all the NLIDBs discussed in this section along a few key dimensions. As can be seen, while an ideal NLIDB should support ad hoc natural language queries, self-improving over the time, taking previous interactions with the user into account either without making any parsing errors or capable of automatically correct them. Despite years of research, existing NLIDBs are still far from perfect. Not surprisingly, so far no commercial database system provides NLQ support. However, this field is also moving fast with strong interest and investment from both the academia and industry, with rapid progression undergoing.

4.6   RELATIONSHIP TO OTHER AREAS

4.6.1   RELATIONSHIP TO QUESTION ANSWERING

As illustrated in Figures 4.38a and 4.38b, on the high level a typical NLIDB system and Question Answer (QA) systems looks almost identical: both take as input a question formulated in natural language and must interpret and translate the question in order to answer it correctly. However, there are several key difference between them: (i) the underlying data of NLIDBs is structured or semi-structured, while that of QA systems is usually unstructured documents, as classic QA systems are IR-based as discussed in Section 2.5; (ii) NLIDBs need to translate a NLQ into formal queries based on languages (e.g., SQL) that are much more expressive than the ones that QA systems needs to translate into for factoid questions (e.g., Boolean keyword); and (iii) the results returned by NLIDBs for a NLQ are direct answers obtained based on the execution of a structured query based on the original question; as such it is relatively difficult for a user to verify the correctness of the results; in contrast, the results returned by a QA system are passages or facts extracted from passages; as such, the user can inspect the passages to determine the correctness of the results. As a result, the tasks of building an NLIDB is typically much more complex and involved than building a QA system.

However, with the emerging of hybrid data management systems such as polystores and data lakes (e.g., Deng et al. 2017, Duggan et al. 2015, Färber et al. 2012, IBM 2018), and the rise of semantic search over unstructured and semi-structured data (Bast et al. 2016, Li et al. 2014b), the line between NLIDBs and QA system is becoming blur: an NLIDB for a hybrid data management needs to generate queries that are suitable to run over all the different underlying data management systems. Similarly, a knowledge-based QA system needs to produce structured queries (Section 2.5). The two-stage design of ATHANA (Section 4.5.7) could be a good starting point for designing NLIDBs for polystores, while knowledge-based QA systems could adapt techniques in building NLIDBs such as those discussed in this book to handle more complex query semantics.

4.6.2   RELATIONSHIP TO SEMANTIC PARSING

As discussed earlier in Section 2.4, semantic parsing [Mooney, 2007] refers to the task of translating natural language into a formal meaning representation on which a machine can act. Conceptually, the task of translating a natural language question into a formal query against the underlying database can be viewed as a specific type of semantic parsing. In another words, building an NLIDB can be regarded as building a special-purpose semantic parser with a formal query language as its meaning representation.

Table 4.5: Summary of notable NLIDB systems

Systems	NLQ Support		Capability		State		Parser Error Handling		Ambiguity Handling		Query Construction		Target Language
	Controlled	Ad Hoc	Fixed	Self-improving	Stateless	Stateful	Auto	Interactive	Auto	Interactive	Pre-defined	Learned	
PRECISE	×		×		×		×*		×		×		SQL
NLPQC	×		×		×						×		SQL
NaLIX	×			×		×*		×		×	×		XQuery^a
FREyA		×*		×*	×			×		×	×		SPARQL
NaLIR	×		×		×		×*	×	×	×	×		SQL
NL2CM	×			×	×				×	×		×	OASSIS-QL
ATHANA		×*	×		×		NA	NA	×		×		OQL
SQLizer		×*	×		×		NA	NA	×		×	×	SQL
Seq2SQL		×*	×		×		NA	NA	×		×		SQL

NA stands for *not applicable*; * indicating limited support

^{a} Schema-Free XQuery Li et al. [2004]

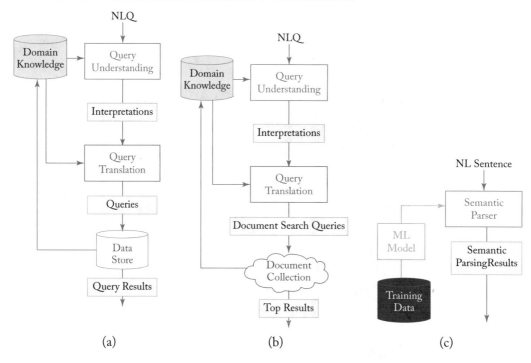

Figure 4.38: Overview of (a) a typical NLIDB system; (b) a typical question answering system; and (c) a typical semantic parser.

However, as can be seen from Figures 4.38a and 4.38c, the current design and implementation of a typical NLIDB system and a typical general-purpose semantic parser differ greatly.

(i) A typical NLIDB system heavily relies on domain knowledge or the knowledge of the underlying data for query understanding and translation; in contrast, a general-purpose semantic parser is usually built in a domain-independent fashion.

(ii) As described in Section 4.5, most NLIDB systems built so far are using deterministic algorithms; in contrast, a typical semantic parser is usually a machine learning model trained with labeled data.

(iii) How to interact with users has been a major design consideration when one builds an NLIDB system, but is rarely a consideration when one builds a general-purpose semantic parser.

In fact, in most cases, a general-purpose semantic parser can be used to help query understanding in an NLIDB system, but the NLIDB system itself still has to do the heavy lifting in query interpretation and generation. It is worth noting, however, that with the increasing attentions on machine learning, the above differences start to change. Several recent NLIDB systems, including SQLizer (Section 4.5.8 and Seq2SQL Section 4.5.9) discussed in this book, have been built by leveraging techniques used in building general-purpose semantic parsers. We refer the readers to Liang [2016] for a more comprehensive overview of the techniques used in building semantic parsers.

4.7   SUMMARY

With the recent surge of voice-based personal assists, such as Apple's Siri, Amazon's Alexa, Microsoft's Cortana, and Google Home, as well as chatbot APIs (e.g., IBM Watson Assistant, Microsoft Bot Framework, Api.ai, etc.), the demand for easier access to data will continue to grow. The landscape of NLIDBs is rapidly changing with reignited interests from the industry as well as academia. As a result, latest techniques developed to solve other artificial intelligence problem, such as deep neural network, has been adapted to provide better NLIDBs with preliminary but promising results. We hope that by surveying existing work and provides a comprehensive and systematic view of the problem space, we can help both researchers and practitioners interested in building NLIDBs to better understand the challenges, leverage existing techniques, and develop ones to address these challenges.

CHAPTER 5

Open Challenges and Opportunities

The progress in natural language processing over the past couple of years has impacted many related areas including machine translation, sentiment analysis, question answering, and information extraction. Database management systems are also affected by these developments, and this book reviews two areas where the progress has been significant: (1) natural language interfaces to databases and (2) natural language data management. The merger of database management and natural language processing introduces many interesting challenges and opportunities, some of which are discussed throughout the book. This chapter reviews a few more fundamental challenges that are relevant to the merger.

5.1 RESOLVING REFERENCES

Relational databases have been traditionally key-oriented; every entity has a key, every relation has a key, and entities are referenced using their keys, giving rise to primary-foreign key relationships between tables. Keys also play a major role even in NoSQL databases (e.g., key-value stores, triple stores, etc.). However, this simple abstraction of an entity in terms of a numeric or a short string key does not carry over to natural languages. It is not uncommon for the same entity to be referenced using multiple ids, and those ids can be ambiguous, referencing multiple entities. This is a problem for both natural language data management and NLIDBs. Without reliable ids, pulling data from different sources and joining them is a challenge. Also NLIDB systems can struggle when there is a vocabulary gap and query references (e.g., for ad hoc queries) do not align well with those in the database being queried. There has been progress in the area of named entity disambiguation, especially when entities are listed in external sources (e.g., Wikipedia pages, RDF resources) [Cucerzan, 2007]. Also record linkage and deduplication has been one of long-standing goals of data integration [Christen, 2012b, Stonebraker and Ilyas, 2018]. Any major progress in named entity disambiguation can impact natural language data management and interfaces.

5.2   UNDERSTANDING NATURAL LANGUAGE TEXT AND QUERIES

Understanding natural languages has been a challenge, often due to all the ambiguities that may be present, the syntax variability that may be allowed and the background knowledge that may be needed. Natural language statements and questions are expressed within a context and understanding or modeling context (or what is known as pragmatic) has been one of the most difficult aspects of NLP. Future research is expected to make progress in areas where contextual information is either less relevant or easily available. The progress in stateless NLIDBs (compared to statefull systems) is an example of this trend.

5.3   MOBILE NATURAL LANGUAGE DATA MANAGEMENT

The number of mobile phone users has been rapidly increasing and is expected to pass the five billion mark by 2019 as predicated by Statista [2018]; with more than half of those users being smart phone users, the scale of content that is being produced or accessed is growing fast. A good portion of this content is in natural language text (e.g., emails, tweets, web pages, documents). Also, the need for conversational, situation-aware NLIDBs on these devices has never been stronger (e.g., Siri, Alexa, Google Assistant, Cortana). Mobile devices bring new challenges in natural language data management due to their limited battery and bandwidth, but they also offer opportunities in terms of additional information that may be available about users and the context in which the interactions are taking place. For example, more than 30% of mobile searches are location-based [Sohn et al., 2008], and NLIDBs can better be geared toward such searches.

5.4   MULTILINGUAL/CROSS-LINGUAL SUPPORT

Much of the work discussed in the book focus on one single language, namely English. Obviously the needs for managing natural languages and building natural language interfaces to databases are universal. Ideally, content with the same semantics but in different languages should be represented in the same abstraction and users should be able to issue queries in different languages against the same underlying database. However, as briefly touched upon in Section 2.2, techniques in language analysis and understanding vary across different languages and most progresses usually happen for English. Providing universal language analysis and understanding as well as interfaces remain open research questions, with notable progress made on universal part-of-speech tagging (e.g., Sylak-Glassman et al. 2015), universal dependency (e.g., Nivre et al. 2016), and universal semantic parsing (e.g., Akbik et al. 2015, Reddy et al. 2017).

5.5   EVALUATION

One obstacle in developing NLIDBs and natural language data management systems is the lack of benchmark(s). Benchmarks have been instrumental in the database community because of an emerging consensus on what needs to be measured and how it should be measured. With no standard benchmark, many studies end up developing their own test suites or using proprietary data, which limits access to the public. An interesting open challenge in natural language data management and interfaces is developing benchmarks that capture different types of workloads that are important for a class of users or applications. In addition, with the rising interest in applying machine learning, in particular deep learning, toward NLIDB, building labeled dataset of sufficient size and complexity is becoming increasingly important for both developing and benchmarking NLIDBs. Recent work [Brad et al., 2017, Trivedi et al., 2017, Zhong et al., 2017] is making some progress in fulfilling the needs.

Besides benchmark dataset, another important aspect of evaluation is evaluation metrics. Manually examining the formal queries generated from NLQ is the most accurate way to measure the correctness of them. However, it is labor intensive and does not scale. One common alternative (e.g., Li and Jagadish 2014, Li et al. 2007b, Saha et al. 2016, Yaghmazadeh et al. 2017) is to compare the results obtained by executing these queries against the expected results. However, the issue is that different queries could generate the same result and thus such metrics could reward the wrongly generated queries. Another alternative (e.g., Brad et al. 2017, Iyer et al. 2017, Xu et al. 2017, Zhong et al. 2017) is to compare the generated queries (or the intermediate logical forms) against the ground truth. However, since the query could be written in different ways, such metrics could mistakenly penalize correctly generated queries based on exact matches (e.g., Zhong et al. 2017), while over-rewarding wrongly generated queries that are syntactically similar to but semantically different from the ground truth (e.g., BLEU [Papineni et al., 2002] used by Brad et al. 2017). Designing the right evaluation metrics that can be automatically evaluated and easily interpreted remains an open challenge.

CHAPTER 6

Conclusions

Addressing the challenges related to natural language, both in terms of data management and interfaces toward databases, is critical to the increasing volume of natural language data and demands for democratizing the access to databases. This book explores the progress that has been made by the database community on the topics of natural language data management and natural language interfaces toward databases. It also presents open challenges and opportunities related to these topics. The book grew out of a three-hour tutorial on the same subject [Li and Rafiei, 2017], given by the authors at SIGMOD 2017.

After a brief introduction in Chapter 1, Chapters 3–4 cover the core topics of natural language data management and natural language interfaces to databases. First, each chapter starts with a quick overview of the topic and identifies related key challenges. Then, subsequent sections in the chapter present detailed discussions on recent innovative techniques that have been proposed to address the challenges. Section 4.5 also presents a few works on building natural language interfaces to databases to highlight design considerations and decisions made by each system. Finally, Chapter 5 describes the open challenges and opportunities that arise in natural language data management and interfaces.

The techniques presented in the book are not intended to be an exhaustive list of works related to natural language data management and interfaces, nor can they be expected to be given the fast-moving pace of this field of research. However, we do hope that this book services as a starting point for those interested in pursuing additional work on these exciting topics and realize the grand vision laid out by Ted Codd nearly half a century ago.

Bibliography

Serge Abiteboul, Dallan Quass, Jason McHugh, Jennifer Widom, and Janet L. Wiener. The lorel query language for semistructured data. *International Journal on Digital Libraries*, 1 (1):68–88, 1997. DOI: 10.1007/s007990050005. 21

Eugene Agichtein and Luis Gravano. Snowball: Extracting relations from large plain-text collections. In *Proc. of the 5th ACM Conference on Digital Libraries*, pages 85–94, 2000. DOI: 10.1145/336597.336644. 46

Eugene Agichtein and Luis Gravano. Querying text databases for efficient information extraction. In *Proc. of the ICDE Conference*, pages 113–124, Bangalore, India, March 2003. DOI: 10.1109/ICDE.2003.1260786. 46

Sanjay Agrawal, Kaushik Chakrabarti, Surajit Chaudhuri, and Venkatesh Ganti. Scalable ad hoc entity extraction from text collections. *PVLDB*, 1(1):945–957, 2008. http://www.vldb .org/pvldb/1/1453958.pdf DOI: 10.14778/1453856.1453958. 46

Alfred V. Aho and Jeffrey D. Ullman. *The Theory of Parsing, Translation, and Compiling*, vol. 1, Prentice-Hall, Englewood Cliffs, NJ, 1972. 8

Alan Akbik, Laura Chiticariu, Marina Danilevsky, Yunyao Li, Shivakumar Vaithyanathan, and Huaiyu Zhu. Generating high quality proposition banks for multilingual semantic role labeling. In *Proc. of the 53rd Annual Meeting of the Association for Computational Linguistics and the 7th International Joint Conference on Natural Language Processing of the Asian Federation of Natural Language Processing, ACL, (Volume 1: Long Papers)*, pages 397–407, Beijing, China, July 26–31, 2015. DOI: 10.3115/v1/p15-1039. 108

James F. Allen, Lenhart K. Schubert, George Ferguson, Peter Heeman, Chung Hee Hwang, Tsuneaki Kato, Marc Light, Nathaniel Martin, Bradford Miller, Massimo Poesio, David R. Traum. The trains project: A case study in building a conversational planning agent. *Journal of Experimental and Theoretical Artificial Intelligence*, 7(1):7–48, 1995. DOI: 10.1080/09528139508953799. 32

Yael Amsterdamer, Susan B. Davidson, Tova Milo, Slava Novgorodov, and Amit Somech. Oassis: Query driven crowd mining. In *SIGMOD4*, pages 589–600, 2014. DOI: 10.1145/2588555.2610514. 85

Yael Amsterdamer, Yael Grossman, Tova Milo, and Pierre Senellart. Crowd mining. In *SIGMOD*, pages 241–252, 2015a. DOI: 10.1145/2463676.2465318. 84

Yael Amsterdamer, Anna Kukliansky, and Tova Milo. A natural language interface for querying general and individual knowledge. *PVLDB*, 8(12):1430–1441, August 2015b. DOI: 10.14778/2824032.2824042. 63, 84

Yael Amsterdamer, Anna Kukliansky, and Tova Milo. A natural language interface for querying general and individual knowledge. *Proc. VLDB Endowment*, 8(12):1430–1441, August 2015c. DOI: 10.14778/2824032.2824042. 84

Daniel Andor, Chris Alberti, David Weiss, Aliaksei Severyn, Alessandro Presta, Kuzman Ganchev, Slav Petrov, and Michael Collins. Globally normalized transition-based neural networks. http://arxiv.org/abs/1603.06042, 2016. DOI: 10.18653/v1/p16-1231. 54

Gabor Angeli, Melvin Jose Johnson Premkumar, and Christopher D. Manning. Leveraging linguistic structure for open domain information extraction. In *Proc. of the 53rd Annual Meeting of the Association for Computational Linguistics and the 7th International Joint Conference on Natural Language Processing (Volume 1: Long Papers)*, pages 344–354, 2015. DOI: 10.3115/v1/p15-1034. 43

Chinatsu Aone, Mary Ellen Okurowski, and James Gorlinsky. Trainable, scalable summarization using robust NLP and machine learning. In *Proc. of the 17th International Conference on Computational Linguistics*, vol. 1, pages 62–66, Association for Computational Linguistics, 1998. DOI: 10.3115/980845.980856. 17

Franz Baader, Ian Horrocks, and Ulrike Sattler. Description logics. *Foundations of Artificial Intelligence*, 3:135–179, 2008. DOI: 10.1007/978-3-540-24750-0_1. 34

H. Bais, M. Machkour, and L. Koutti. Querying database using a universal natural language interface based on machine learning. In *IT4OD*, 2016. DOI: 10.1109/IT4OD.2016.7479304. 50, 63

Collin F. Baker, Charles J. Fillmore, and John B. Lowe. The Berkeley framenet project. In *Proc. of the 17th International Conference on Computational Linguistics (COLING)*, vol. 1, pages 86–90, Association for Computational Linguistics, Stroudsburg, PA, 1998. DOI: 10.3115/980451.980860. 10, 20, 37

Laura Banarescu, Claire Bonial, Shu Cai, Madalina Georgescu, Kira Griffitt, Ulf Hermjakob, Kevin Knight, Philipp Koehn, Martha Palmer, and Nathan Schneider. Abstract meaning representation for sembanking. In *LAW@ACL*, 2013. 8

Michele Banko, Michael J. Cafarella, Stephen Soderland, Matthew Broadhead, and Oren Etzioni. Open information extraction from the Web. In *IJCAI*, vol. 7, pages 2670–2676, 2007. DOI: 10.1145/1409360.1409378. 43

Hannah Bast, Buchhold Björn, and Elmar Haussmann. Semantic search on text and knowledge bases. *Foundations and Trends in Information Retrieval*, 10(2–3):119–271, June 2016. DOI: 10.1561/1500000032. 102

Yoshua Bengio, Réjean Ducharme, Pascal Vincent, and Christian Jauvin. A neural probabilistic language model. *Journal of Machine Learning Research*, 3:1137–1155, February 2003. DOI: 10.1007/10985687_6. 36

Jonathan Berant and Percy Liang. Semantic parsing via paraphrasing. In *ACL (1)*, pages 1415–1425, 2014. DOI: 10.3115/v1/P14-1133. 94

J. Bhogal, A. Macfarlane, and P. Smith. A review of ontology based query expansion. *Information Processing and Management*, 43(4):866–886, July 2007. DOI: 10.1016/j.ipm.2006.09.003. 58

Steven Bird, Yi Chen, Susan B. Davidson, Haejoong Lee, and Yifeng Zheng. Designing and evaluating an Xpath dialect for linguistic queries. In *Proc. of the ICDE Conference*, pages 52–52, IEEE, 2006. DOI: 10.1109/icde.2006.48. 28

Florin Brad, Radu Iacob, Ionel Hosu, and Traian Rebedea. Dataset for a neural natural language interface for databases (NNLIDB). In *IJCNLP*, 2017. 65, 109

Thorsten Brants. TNT: a statistical part-of-speech tagger. In *Proc. of the 6th Conference on Applied Natural Language Processing*, pages 224–231, Association for Computational Linguistics, 2000. DOI: 10.3115/974147.974178. 6

Sergey Brin. Extracting patterns and relations from the World Wide Web. In *International Workshop on the World Wide Web and Databases*, pages 172–183, Springer, 1998. 46

Razvan Bunescu and Raymond J. Mooney. Collective information extraction with relational Markov networks. In *Proc. of the 42nd Annual Meeting on Association for Computational Linguistics*, page 438, 2004. DOI: 10.3115/1218955.1219011. 42

Razvan Bunescu and Marius Paşca. Using encyclopedic knowledge for named entity disambiguation. In *11th Conference of the European Chapter of the Association for Computational Linguistics*, 2006. 44

Michael J. Cafarella and Oren Etzioni. A search engine for natural language applications. In *Proc. of the 14th International Conference on World Wide Web*, pages 442–452, ACM, 2005. DOI: 10.1145/1060745.1060811. 26

Xavier Carreras and Lluís Màrquez. Introduction to the CoNLL-2005 shared task: Semantic role labeling. In *Proc. of the 9th Conference on Computational Natural Language Learning*, pages 152–164, Association for Computational Linguistics, 2005. 45

Stefano Ceri, Georg Gottlob, and Letizia Tanca. What you always wanted to know about datalog (and never dared to ask). *IEEE Transactions on Knowledge and Data Engineering*, 1(1):146–166, 1989. DOI: 10.1109/69.43410. 22

Eugene Charniak. A maximum-entropy-inspired parser. In *NAACL*, 2000. 68

Surajit Chaudhuri, Umeshwar Dayal, and Tak W. Yan. Join queries with external text sources: Execution and optimization techniques. In *ACM SIGMOD Record*, pages 410–422, San Jose, CA, May 1995. DOI: 10.1145/223784.223856. 46

Hai Leong Chieu, Hwee Tou Ng, and Yoong Keok Lee. Closing the gap: Learning-based information extraction rivaling knowledge-engineering methods. In *Proc. of the 41st Annual Meeting on Association for Computational Linguistics*, vol. 1, pages 216–223, 2003. 42, 43

Nancy Chinchor. Overview of MUC-7. In *7th Message Understanding Conference (MUC-7): Proceedings of a Conference*, Fairfax, VA, April 29–May 1, 1998. 42

Laura Chiticariu, Yunyao Li, Sriram Raghavan, and Frederick R. Reiss. Enterprise information extraction: Recent developments and open challenges. In *Proc. of the ACM SIGMOD International Conference on Management of Data*, pages 1257–1258, 2010. DOI: 10.1145/1807167.1807339. 43

Laura Chiticariu, Yunyao Li, and Frederick R. Reiss. Rule-based information extraction is dead! Long live rule-based information extraction systems! In *Proc. of the Conference on Empirical Methods in Natural Language Processing*, pages 827–832, 2013. 1, 43

Peter Christen. *Data Matching: Concepts and Techniques for Record Linkage, Entity Resolution, and Duplicate Detection*, Springer Science and Business Media, 2012a. DOI: 10.1007/978-3-642-31164-2. 16

Peter Christen. A survey of indexing techniques for scalable record linkage and deduplication. *IEEE Transactions on Knowledge and Data Engineering*, 24(9):1537–1555, 2012b. DOI: 10.1109/TKDE.2011.127. 107

Vassilis Christophides, Serge Abiteboul, Sophie Cluet, and Michel Scholl. From structured documents to novel query facilities. *ACM SIGMOD Record*, 23(2):313–324, 1994. DOI: 10.1145/191843.191901. 21

Eric Chu, Akanksha Baid, Ting Chen, AnHai Doan, and Jeffrey Naughton. A relational approach to incrementally extracting and querying structure in unstructured data. In *Proc. of the VLDB Conference*, 2007. 46

Pirooz Chubak and Davood Rafiei. Index structures for efficiently searching natural language text. In *Proc. of the CIKM Conference*, pages 689–698, ACM, 2010. DOI: 10.1145/1871437.1871527. 26, 28

Pirooz Chubak and Davood Rafiei. Efficient indexing and querying over syntactically annotated trees. *Proc. of the VLDB Endowment*, 5(11):1316–1327, 2012. DOI: 10.14778/2350229.2350249. 29, 30, 32

E. F. Codd. Relational completeness of data base sublanguages. In *Database Systems*, pages 65–98, Prentice Hall, 1972. 65

E. F. Codd. Seven steps to rendezvous with the casual user. In *IFIP Working Conference Data Base Management*, pages 179–200, 1974. 1

Michael Collins. Three generative, lexicalised models for statistical parsing. In *Proc. of the 8th Conference on European Chapter of the Association for Computational Linguistics*, pages 16–23, 1997. 8

Michael Collins. Head-driven statistical models for natural language parsing. *Computational Linguistics*, 29(4):589–637, 2003. 8

Michael John Collins. A new statistical parser based on bigram lexical dependencies. In *Proc. of the 34th Annual Meeting on Association for Computational Linguistics*, pages 184–191, 1996. 17

Mathias Creutz and Krista Lagus. Unsupervised models for morpheme segmentation and morphology learning. *ACM Transactions on Speech and Language Processing (TSLP)*, 4(1):3, 2007. DOI: 10.1145/1187415.1187418. 6

Silviu Cucerzan. Large-scale named entity disambiguation based on Wikipedia data. In *Proc. of the Joint Conference on Empirical Methods in Natural Language Processing and Computational Natural Language Learning (EMNLP-CoNLL)*, 2007. 44, 45, 107

Bhavana Dalvi, Sumithra Bhakthavatsalam, Chris Clark, Peter Clark, Oren Etzioni, Anthony Fader, and Dirk Groeneveld. Ike-an interactive tool for knowledge extraction. In *Proc. of the 5th Workshop on Automated Knowledge Base Construction*, pages 12–17, 2016. DOI: 10.18653/v1/w16-1303. 22

Danica Damljanovic, Valentin Tablan, and Kalina Bontcheva. A text-based query interface to owl ontologies. In *LREC*, 2008. 79

Danica Damljanovic, Milan Agatonovic, and Hamish Cunningham. Freya: An interactive way of querying linked data using natural language. In *ESWC*, pages 125–138, 2012. DOI: 10.1007/978-3-642-25953-1_11. 63, 79, 82

Danica Damljanovic, Milan Agatonovic, Hamish Cunningham, and Kalina Bontcheva. Improving habitability of natural language interfaces for querying ontologies with feedback and clarification dialogues. *Journal of Web Semantics*, 19:1–21, 2013a. DOI: 10.2139/ssrn.3198998. 63, 79

Danica Damljanovic, Milan Agatonovic, Hamish Cunningham, and Kalina Bontcheva. Improving habitability of natural language interfaces for querying ontologies with feedback and clarification dialogues. *Journal of Web Semantics*, 19:1–21, 2013b. DOI: 10.2139/ssrn.3198998. 79

Marie-Catherine de Marneffe, Bill MacCartney, and Christopher D. Manning. Generating typed dependency parses from phrase structure parses. In *LREC*, 2006. 85

Marie-Catherine de Marneffe, Bill MacCartney, Christopher D. Manning, et al. Generating typed dependency parses from phrase structure parses. In *Proc. of LREC*, pages 449–454, Genoa Italy, 2006. 8

Dong Deng, Raul Castro Fernandez, Ziawasch Abedjan, Sibo Wang, Michael Stonebraker, Ahmed K. Elmagarmid, Ihab F. Ilyas, Samuel Madden, Mourad Ouzzani, and Nan Tang. The data civilizer system. In *CIDR*, 2017. 102

AnHai Doan, Raghu Ramakrishnan, and Shivakumar Vaithyanathan. Managing information extraction: State of the art and research directions. In *Proc. of the ACM SIGMOD International Conference on Management of Data*, pages 799–800, ACM, 2006. DOI: 10.1145/1142473.1142595. 43

Jennie Duggan, Aaron J. Elmore, Michael Stonebraker, Magda Balazinska, Bill Howe, Jeremy Kepner, Sam Madden, David Maier, Tim Mattson, and Stan Zdonik. The bigdawg polystore system. *SIGMOD Record*, 44(2):11–16, August 2015. DOI: 10.1145/2814710.2814713. 102

Greg Durrett and John DeNero. Supervised learning of complete morphological paradigms. In *Proc. of the Conference of the North American Chapter of the Association for Computational Linguistics: Human Language Technologies*, pages 1185–1195, 2013. 7

Jeffrey L. Elman. Finding structure in time. *Cognitive Science*, 14(2):179–211, 1990. DOI: 10.1207/s15516709cog1402_1. 53

Oren Etzioni, Anthony Fader, Janara Christensen, Stephen Soderland, and Mausam Mausam. Open information extraction: The second generation. In *IJCAI*, vol. 11, pages 3–10, 2011. DOI: 10.5591/978-1-57735-516-8/IJCAI11-012. 43

Anthony Fader, Stephen Soderland, and Oren Etzioni. Identifying relations for open information extraction. In *Proc. of the Conference on Empirical Methods in Natural Language Processing*, pages 1535–1545, Association for Computational Linguistics, 2011. 43

Franz Färber, Sang Kyun Cha, Jürgen Primsch, Christof Bornhövd, Stefan Sigg, and Wolfgang Lehner. Sap Hana database: Data management for modern business applications. *SIGMOD Record*, 40(4):45–51, January 2012. DOI: 10.1145/2094114.2094126. 102

David Ferrucci. Build Watson: An overview of deepqa for the jeopardy! challenge. In *Proc. of the 19th International Conference on Parallel Architectures and Compilation Techniques, (PACT)*, pages 1–2, New York, ACM, 2010. DOI: 10.1145/1854273.1854275. 10

David A. Ferrucci. Introduction to "this is Watson." *IBM Journal of Research and Development*, 56(3.4):1–1, 2012. 2

Victoria Fromkin and Rodman Robert. *Introduction to Language*, 10th ed. Wadsworth Publishing, 2013. 58

Eugene Garfield. The permuterm subject index: An autobiographical review. *Journal of the Association for Information Science and Technology*, 27(5):288–291, 1976. DOI: 10.1002/asi.4630270504. 26

Daniel Gildea and Daniel Jurafsky. Automatic labeling of semantic roles. *Computational Linguistics*, 28(3):245–288, 2002. 41

Alessandra Giordani and Alessandro Moschitti. Translating questions to SQL queries with generative parsers discriminatively reranked. In *COLING*, pages 401–410, 2012. 65

G. H. Gonnet and F. Wm Tompa. Mind your grammar: A new approach to text databases. In *Proc. of the VLDB Conference*, pages 339–346, 1987. 21

Swapna Gottipati and Jing Jiang. Linking entities to a knowledge base with query expansion. In *Proc. of the Conference on Empirical Methods in Natural Language Processing*, pages 804–813, Association for Computational Linguistics, 2011. 44

Roberto Grossi, Ankur Gupta, and Jeffrey Scott Vitter. High-order entropy-compressed text indexes. In *Proc. of the 14th Annual ACM-SIAM Symposium on Discrete Algorithms*, pages 841–850, Society for Industrial and Applied Mathematics, 2003. 28

Luheng He, Kenton Lee, Mike Lewis, and Luke Zettlemoyer. Deep semantic role labeling: What works and what's next. In *Proc. of the 55th Annual Meeting of the Association for Computational Linguistics (Volume 1: Long Papers)*, vol. 1, pages 473–483, 2017a. DOI: 10.18653/v1/p17-1044. 45

Luheng He, Kenton Lee, Mike Lewis, and Luke S. Zettlemoyer. Deep semantic role labeling: What works and what's next. In *ACL*, 2017b. DOI: 10.18653/v1/p17-1044. 10

Marti A. Hearst. Automatic acquisition of hyponyms from large text corpora. In *Proc. of the COLING Conference*, pages 539–545, Association for Computational Linguistics, 1992. DOI: 10.3115/992133.992154. 23

Charles T. Hemphill, John J. Godfrey, and George R. Doddington. The ATIS spoken language systems pilot corpus. In *Proc. of the Speech and Natural Language*, Hidden Valley, PA, June 24–27, 1990. DOI: 10.3115/116580.116613. 53

IBM. IBM DB2 Hybrid Data Management, 2018. 102

Srinivasan Iyer, Ioannis Konstas, Alvin Cheung, Jayant Krishnamurthy, and Luke Zettlemoyer. Learning a neural semantic parser from user feedback. In *ACL*, pages 963–973, 2017. DOI: 10.18653/v1/p17-1089. 65, 109

Paul Jaccard. Distribution de la flore alpine dans le bassin des dranses et dans quelques régions voisines. *Bulletin de la Société Vaudoise des Sciences Naturelles*, 37:241–272, 1901. DOI: 10.5169/seals-266440. 62

Alpa Jain, AnHai Doan, and Luis Gravano. Optimizing SQL queries over text databases. In *Proc. of the ICDE Conference*, pages 636–645, Cancun, Mexico, April 2008. DOI: 10.1109/ICDE.2008.4497472. 46

Kristina Jokinen and Michael McTear. *Spoken Dialogue Systems*, Morgan & Claypool Publishers, 2010. DOI: 10.2200/S00204ED1V01Y200910HLT005. 13

John Judge, Aoife Cahill, and Josef van Genabith. Questionbank: Creating a corpus of parse-annotated questions. In *ACL*, 2006. DOI: 10.3115/1220175.1220238. 54

Daniel Jurafsky and James H. Martin. *Speech and Language Processing*, 2nd ed. Prentice-Hall, Inc., Upper Saddle River, NJ, 2009a. 8, 13

Daniel Jurafsky and James H. Martin. *Speech and Language Processing*, Prentice Hall, Inc., Upper Saddle River, NJ, 2009b. 5, 52

Ehsan Kamalloo and Davood Rafiei. A coherent unsupervised model for toponym resolution. In *Proc. of the World Wide Web Conference on World Wide Web*, pages 1287–1296, International World Wide Web Conferences Steering Committee, 2018. 44

Paul Kingsbury and Martha Palmer. From treebank to propbank. In *LREC*, pages 1989–1993, Citeseer, 2002. 37

Karin Kipper, Anna Korhonen, Neville Ryant, and Martha Palmer. Extending verbnet with novel verb classes. In *LREC*, 2006. 41

Andreas Kokkalis, Panagiotis Vagenas, Alexandros Zervakis, Alkis Simitsis, Georgia Koutrika, and Yannis E. Ioannidis. Logos: A system for translating queries into narratives. In *Proc. of the ACM SIGMOD International Conference on Management of Data*, pages 673–676, 2012. DOI: 10.1145/2213836.2213929. 60

Sandra Kubler, Ryan McDonald, Joakim Nivre, and Graeme Hirst. *Dependency Parsing*, Morgan & Claypool Publishers, 2009. DOI: 10.2200/s00169ed1v01y200901hlt002. 54

Sayali Kulkarni, Amit Singh, Ganesh Ramakrishnan, and Soumen Chakrabarti. Collective annotation of Wikipedia entities in web text. In *Proc. of the 15th ACM SIGKDD International Conference on Knowledge Discovery and Data Mining*, pages 457–466, ACM, 2009. DOI: 10.1145/1557019.1557073. 44

Quoc Le and Tomas Mikolov. Distributed representations of sentences and documents. In *International Conference on Machine Learning*, pages 1188–1196, 2014. 42

Jochen L. Leidner et al. Toponym resolution in text:"Which sheffield is it?" In *Proc. of the 27th Annual International ACM SIGIR Conference (SIGIR)*, page 602, 2004. DOI: 10.1145/1008992.1009147. 46

Michael Lesk. Automatic sense disambiguation using machine readable dictionaries: How to tell a pine cone from an ice cream cone. In *Proc. of the 5th Annual International Conference on Systems Documentation*, pages 24–26, ACM, 1986. DOI: 10.1145/318723.318728. 38

Beth Levin. *English Verb Classes and Alternations: A Preliminary Investigation*, University of Chicago Press, 1993. 40

Fei Li and H. V. Jagadish. Constructing an interactive natural language interface for relational databases. *PVLDB*, 8(1):73–84, 2014. DOI: 10.14778/2735461.2735468. 50, 55, 58, 59, 60, 63, 66, 67, 82, 109

Fei Li, Tianyin Pan, and H. V. Jagadish. Schema-free SQL. In *SIGMOD*, pages 1051–1062, 2014a. DOI: 10.1145/2588555.2588571. 61

Huadong Li, Yafang Wang, Gerard de Melo, Changhe Tu, and Baoquan Chen. Multimodal question answering over structured data with ambiguous entities. In *Proc. of the 26th International Conference on World Wide Web Companion, (WWW)*, pages 79–88, International World Wide Web Conferences Steering Committee, Republic and Canton of Geneva, Switzerland, 2017. DOI: 10.1145/3041021.3054135. 11

Yunyao Li and Davood Rafiei. Natural language data management and interfaces: Recent development and open challenges. In *Proc. of the ACM International Conference on Management of Data*, pages 1765–1770, 2017. DOI: 10.1145/3035918.3054783. xviii, 111

Yunyao Li, Cong Yu, and H. V. Jagadish. Schema-free Xquery. In *VLDB*, pages 72–83, 2004. DOI: 10.1016/B978-012088469-8.50010-3. 61, 73, 76

Yunyao Li, Huahai Yang, and H. V. Jagadish. Constructing a generic natural language interface for an XML database. In *Proc. of the EDBT Conference*, pages 737–754, 2006. DOI: 10.1007/11687238_44. 47, 51, 55, 59, 60, 73

Yunyao Li, Ishan Chaudhuri, Huahai Yang, Satinder Singh, and H. V. Jagadish. Enabling domain-awareness for a generic natural language interface. In *AAAI*, pages 833–838, 2007a. 54, 55, 59, 63, 73, 74

Yunyao Li, Huahai Yang, and H. V. Jagadish. Nalix: A generic natural language search environment for XML data. *ACM Transactions on Database Systems*, 32(4), 2007b. DOI: 10.1145/1292609.1292620. 51, 53, 55, 58, 59, 60, 63, 67, 73, 74, 75, 78, 109

Yunyao Li, Ziyang Liu, and Huaiyu Zhu. Enterprise search in the big data era: Recent developments and open challenges. *PVLDB*, 7(13):1717–1718, 2014b. DOI: 10.14778/2733004.2733071. 89, 102

Percy Liang. Learning executable semantic parsers for natural language understanding. *Communications on ACM*, 59(9), August 2016. DOI: 10.1145/2866568. 47, 49, 105

Dekang Lin. Automatic retrieval and clustering of similar words. In *ACL*, pages 768–774, 1998a. DOI: 10.3115/980432.980696. 40

Dekang Lin. Dependency-based evaluation of minipar. In *Proc. of the Workshop on the Evaluation of Parsing Systems*, 1998b. DOI: 10.1007/978-94-010-0201-1_18. 73

Dekang Lin and Patrick Pantel. Discovery of inference rules for question-answering. *Natural Language Engineering*, 7(4):343–360, 2001. DOI: 10.1017/S1351324901002765. 16, 17

Dekang Lin, Shaojun Zhao, Lijuan Qin, and Ming Zhou. Identifying synonyms among distributionally similar words. In *IJCAI*, vol. 3, pages 1492–1493, 2003. 16, 22

Dekang Lin et al. An information-theoretic definition of similarity. In *ICML*, 1998. 39

Yuri Lin, Jean-Baptiste Michel, Erez Lieberman Aiden, Jon Orwant, Will Brockman, and Slav Petrov. Syntactic annotations for the Google books ngram corpus. In *Proc. of the ACL System Demonstrations*, pages 169–174, 2012. 17

Julie Beth Lovins. Development of a stemming algorithm. *Translation and Computational Linguistics*, 11(1):22–31, 1968. 57

W. S. Luk and Steve Kloster. Elfs: English language from SQL. *ACM Transactions on Database Systems*, 11(4):447–472, December 1986. DOI: 10.1145/7239.384276. 93

Christopher D. Manning, Prabhakar Raghavan, and Hinrich Schütze. *Introduction to Information Retrieval*, Cambridge University Press, 2008. DOI: 10.1017/CBO9780511809071. 57

Christopher D. Manning, Mihai Surdeanu, John Bauer, Jenny Rose Finkel, Steven Bethard, and David McClosky. The Stanford CoreNLP natural language processing toolkit. In *ACL (System Demonstrations)*, pages 55–60, 2014. DOI: 10.3115/v1/p14-5010. 17, 94, 101

Adam Marcus and Aditya Parameswaran. Crowdsourced data management: Industry and academic perspectives. *Foundations in Trends databases*, 6(1–2), December 2015. 84

Mitchell P. Marcus, Mary Ann Marcinkiewicz, and Beatrice Santorini. Building a large annotated corpus of English: The penn treebank. *Computational linguistics*, 19(2):313–330, 1993. DOI: 10.21236/ada273556. 5, 17

Cynthia Matuszek, Evan Herbst, Luke Zettlemoyer, and Dieter Fox. *Learning to Parse Natural Language Commands to a Robot Control System*, pages 403–415, Springer International Publishing, Heidelberg, 2013. DOI: 10.1007/978–3-319-00065-7_28. 8

Mikaël Mayer, Gustavo Soares, Maxim Grechkin, Vu Le, Mark Marron, Oleksandr Polozov, Rishabh Singh, Benjamin Zorn, and Sumit Gulwani. User interaction models for disambiguation in programming by example. In *UIST*, 2015. DOI: 10.1145/2807442.2807459. 67

Andrew McCallum, Dayne Freitag, and Fernando C. N. Pereira. Maximum entropy Markov models for information extraction and segmentation. In *ICML*, pages 591–598, 2000. 43

Tomas Mikolov, Ilya Sutskever, Kai Chen, Greg Corrado, and Jeffrey Dean. Distributed representations of words and phrases and their compositionality. In *NIPS*, 2013a. 58

Tomas Mikolov, Ilya Sutskever, Kai Chen, Greg S. Corrado, and Jeff Dean. Distributed representations of words and phrases and their compositionality. In *Advances in Neural Information Processing Systems*, pages 3111–3119, 2013b. 36, 42

George A. Miller. Wordnet: A lexical database for English. *Communications of the ACM*, 38(11):39–41, 1995a. DOI: 10.1145/219717.219748. 36

George A. Miller. WordNet: A lexical database for English. *Communications of the ACM*, 38(11):39–41, 1995b. DOI: 10.1145/219717.219748. 58, 72, 76

Jeff Mitchell and Mirella Lapata. Composition in distributional models of semantics. *Cognitive Science*, 34(8):1388–1429, 2010. DOI: 10.1111/j.1551-6709.2010.01106.x. 42

Alvaro Monge and Charles Elkan. An efficient domain-independent algorithm for detecting approximately duplicate database records. In *Workshop on Research Issues on Data Mining and Knowledge Discovery*, 1997. 81

Raymond J. Mooney. Learning for semantic parsing. In *CICLing*, 2007. DOI: 10.1007/978-3-540-70939-8_28. 8, 102

Johanna D. Moore. *Participating in Explanatory Dialogues Interpreting and Responding to Questions in Context*, MIT Press, Cambridge, MA, 1995. 51

Joakim Nivre, Marie-Catherine de Marneffe, Filip Ginter, Yoav Goldberg, Jan Hajic, Christopher D. Manning, Ryan T. McDonald, Slav Petrov, Sampo Pyysalo, Natalia Silveira, Reut Tsarfaty, and Daniel Zeman. Universal dependencies v1: A multilingual treebank collection. In *Proc. of the 10th International Conference on Language Resources and Evaluation LREC*, Portorož, Slovenia, May 23–28, 2016. 108

Peter Norvig. Natural language corpus data: Beautiful data. `http://norvig.com/ngrams`, 2017. 17

G. M. Olson, S. A. Duffy, and R. L. Mack. Question-asking as a component of text comprehension. In Arthur C. Graesser and John B. Black, Eds., *The Psychology of Questions*, pages 219–226, Lawrence Erlbaum Associates, Hillsdale, NJ, 1985. 51

Chris D. Paice. Another stemmer. *SIGIR Forum*, 24(3):56–61, 1990. DOI: 10.1145/101306.101310. 57

Ashish Palakurthi, Ruthu S. M., Arjun Akula, and Radhika Mamidi. Classification of attributes in a natural language query into different SQL clauses. In *Recent Advances in Natural Language Processing, RANLP*, pages 497–506, Hissar, Bulgaria, September 7–9, 2015. 64

Martha Palmer. VerbNet: A class-based verb lexicon. `http://verbs.colorado.edu/~mpal mer/projects/verbnet.html`, 2018. 40

Martha Palmer, Daniel Gildea, and Paul Kingsbury. The proposition bank: An annotated corpus of semantic roles. *Computational Linguistics*, 31(1):71–106, 2005. DOI: 10.1162/0891201053630264. 10

Martha Palmer, Daniel Gildea, and Nianwen Xue. *Semantic Role Labeling*, Morgan & Claypool Publishers, 2010a. DOI: 10.2200/S00239ED1V01Y200912HLT006. 8

Martha Palmer, Daniel Gildea, and Nianwen Xue. Semantic role labeling. *Synthesis Lectures on Human Language Technologies*, 3(1):1–103, 2010b. DOI: 10.2200/s00239ed1v01y200912hlt006. 41, 45

Kishore Papineni, Salim Roukos, Todd Ward, and Wei-Jing Zhu. Bleu: A method for automatic evaluation of machine translation. In *ACL*, 2002. DOI: 10.3115/1073083.1073135. 109

Paramount Pictures. Star Trek: The next generation, 1987. 47

Eileen Peacock, Thomas W. Lauer, and Arthur C. Graesser. *Questions and Information Systems*, Lawrence Erlbaum Associates, Mahwah, NJ, 1992. 51

Fuchun Peng and Andrew McCallum. Information extraction from research papers using conditional random fields. *Information Processing and Management*, 42(4):963–979, 2006. DOI: 10.1016/j.ipm.2005.09.002. 43

Sundar Pichai. Google says its speech recognition technology now has only an 8% word error rate. `https://venturebeat.com/2015/05/28/google-says-its-speech-recognition-technology-now-has-only-an-8-word-error-rate/`, 2015. 18

M. Pinkal. Vagueness, ambiguity, and underspecification. In *Proc. of SALT VI*, 1996. 60

Ana-Maria Popescu, Oren Etzioni, and Henry Kautz. Towards a theory of natural language interfaces to databases. In *Proc. of the 8th International Conference on Intelligent User Interfaces, (IUI)*, pages 149–157, 2003. DOI: 10.1145/604045.604120. 49, 54, 58, 68

Ana-maria Popescu, Alex Armanasu, Oren Etzioni, David Ko, and Alexander Yate. Modern natural language interfaces to databases: Composing statistical parsing with semantic tractability. In *COLING*, 2004. DOI: 10.3115/1220355.1220376. 50, 54, 68

Martin F. Porter. An algorithm for suffix stripping. *Program*, 14(3):130–137, 1980. DOI: 10.1108/eb046814. 57

P. J. Price. Evaluation of spoken language systems: The ATIS domain. In *Proc. of the Workshop on Speech and Natural Language, (HLT)*, pages 91–95, 1990. DOI: 10.3115/116580.116612. 71

James Pustejovsky, Patrick Hanks, Roser Sauri, Andrew See, Robert Gaizauskas, Andrea Setzer, Dragomir Radev, Beth Sundheim, David Day, Lisa Ferro, et al. The timebank corpus. In *Corpus Linguistics*, page 40, Lancaster, UK, 2003. 45

Kun Qian, Nikita Bhutani, Yunyao Li, H. V. Jagadish, and Mauricio A. Hernandez. Lustre: An interactive system for entity structured representation and variant generation. In *ICDE*, 2018. 58

Meng Qu, Xiang Ren, and Jiawei Han. Automatic synonym discovery with knowledge bases. In *Proc. of the 23rd ACM SIGKDD International Conference on Knowledge Discovery and Data Mining*, pages 997–1005, 2017. DOI: 10.1145/3097983.3098185. 22

Davood Rafiei and Haobin Li. Data extraction from the Web using wild card queries. In *Proc. of the 18th ACM Conference on Information and Knowledge Management*, pages 1939–1942, 2009a. DOI: 10.1145/1645953.1646270. 21

Davood Rafiei and Haobin Li. Wild card queries for searching resources on the Web. *ArXiv Preprint ArXiv:0908.2588*, 2009b. 21

Jiangwei Yu Rafiei and Davood Rafiei. Geotagging named entities in news and online documents. In *Proc. of the 25th ACM International on Conference on Information and Knowledge Management*, pages 1321–1330, 2016. DOI: 10.1145/2983323.2983795. 46

B. Randall. CorpusSearch Users Manual, University of Pennsylvania. http://www.ling.upenn.edu/~dringe/CorpStuff/Manual/Contents.html 25

Siva Reddy, Oscar Täckström, Slav Petrov, Mark Steedman, and Mirella Lapata. Universal semantic parsing. In *Proc. of the Conference on Empirical Methods in Natural Language Processing, EMNLP*, pages 89–101, Copenhagen, Denmark, September 9–11, 2017. DOI: 10.18653/v1/d17-1009. 108

Hans Reichenbach. *Elements of Symbolic Logic*, Macmilan, 1947. 35

Philip Resnik. Semantic classes and syntactic ambiguity. In *Proc. of the Workshop on Human Language Technology*, pages 278–283, Association for Computational Linguistics, 1993. DOI: 10.3115/1075671.1075733. 42

Philip Resnik. Using information content to evaluate semantic similarity in a taxonomy. In *Proc. of the IJCAI Conference*, pages 448–453, Morgan Kaufmann Publishers Inc., 1995. 39

An Open Language Data Community Resource. Manually annotated sub-corpus (masc). http://www.anc.org/data/masc/downloads/data-download, 2017. 17

D. Rhode. Tgrep2 user manual (version 1.15). https://tedlab.mit.edu/~dr/Tgrep2 25

Diptikalyan Saha, Avrilia Floratou, Karthik Sankaranarayanan, Umar Farooq Minhas, Ashish R. Mittal, and Fatma Özcan. Athena: An ontology-driven system for natural language querying over relational data stores. *PVLDB*, 9(12):1209–1220, August 2016. DOI: 10.14778/2994509.2994536. 58, 59, 61, 63, 66, 67, 87, 91, 93, 109

Hassan Sajjad, Patrick Pantel, and Michael Gamon. Underspecified query refinement via natural language question generation. In *SIGPARSE*, December 2012. 59

K. Shabaz, Jim D. O'Shea, Keeley A. Crockett, and A. Latham. Aneesah: A conversational natural language interface to databases. In *World Congress on Engineering*, pages 227–232, 2015. 63

Dennis Shasha, Jason Tsong-Li Wang, Huiyuan Shan, and Kaizhong Zhang. Atreegrep: Approximate searching in unordered trees. In *Proc. of Scientific and Statistical Database Management*, pages 89–98, IEEE, 2002. DOI: 10.1109/SSDM.2002.1029709. 28

Wei Shen, Jianyong Wang, and Jiawei Han. Entity linking with a knowledge base: Issues, techniques, and solutions. *IEEE Transactions on Knowledge and Data Engineering*, 27(2):443–460, 2015. DOI: 10.1109/TKDE.2014.2327028. 44

Daniel Sleator and Davy Temperly. Parsing English with a link grammar. In *3rd International Workshop on Parsing Technologies*, 1993. 71

Richard Socher, Cliff C. Lin, Chris Manning, and Andrew Y. Ng. Parsing natural scenes and natural language with recursive neural networks. In *Proc. of the 28th International Conference on Machine Learning (ICML)*, pages 129–136, 2011. 42

Timothy Sohn, Kevin A. Li, William G. Griswold, and James D. Hollan. A diary study of mobile information needs. In *Proc. of the SIGCHI Conference on Human Factors in Computing Systems*, pages 433–442, ACM, 2008. DOI: 10.1145/1357054.1357125. 108

Armando Solar-Lezama, Liviu Tancau, Rastislav Bodik, Sanjit Seshia, and Vijay Saraswat. Combinatorial sketching for finite programs. In *ASPLOS*, 2006. DOI: 10.1145/1168918.1168907. 94

Statista. Number of mobile phone users worldwide from 2013–2019 (in billions). https://www.statista.com/statistics/274774/forecast-of-mobile-phone-users-worldwide, 2018. 108

Michael Stonebraker and Ihab F. Ilyas. Data integration: The current status and the way forward. *IEEE Data Engineering Bulletin*, 41(2):3–9, 2018. 107

Niculae Stratica, Leila Kosseim, and Bipin C. Desai. Using semantic templates for a natural language interface to the cindi virtual library. *Data and Knowledge Engineering*, 55(1):4–19, October 2005. DOI: 10.1016/j.datak.2004.12.002. 51, 64, 71

Fabian M. Suchanek, Gjergji Kasneci, and Gerhard Weikum. Yago: A core of semantic knowledge. In *Proc. of the 16th International Conference on World Wide Web*, pages 697–706, ACM, 2007. DOI: 10.1145/1242572.1242667. 2, 44

Fabian M. Suchanek, Mauro Sozio, and Gerhard Weikum. Sofie: A self-organizing framework for information extraction. In *Proc. of the 18th International Conference on World wide web*, pages 631–640, ACM, 2009. DOI: 10.1145/1526709.1526794. 46

Paul Suganthan G. C., Chong Sun, Krishna Gayatri K., Haojun Zhang, Frank Yang, Narasimhan Rampalli, Shishir Prasad, Esteban Arcaute, Ganesh Krishnan, Rohit Deep, Vijay Raghavendra, and AnHai Doan. Why big data industrial systems need rules and what we can do about it. In *Proc. of the ACM SIGMOD International Conference on Management of Data, (SIGMOD)*, pages 265–276, New York, 2015. 1

Alane Suhr, Srinivasan Iyer, and Yoav Artzi. Learning to map context-dependent sentences to executable formal queries. In *Proc. of the Conference of the North American Chapter of the Association for Computational Linguistics: Human Language Technologies, (Volume 1, Long Papers)*, pages 2238–2249, 2018. http://aclweb.org/anthology/N18--1203 DOI: 10.18653/v1/N18-1203 . 53, 65

B. Sujatha, S. Viswanadha Raju, and Humera Shaziya. A survey of natural language interface to database management system. *International Journal of Science and Advanced Technology*, 2(6), 2012. 47, 68

Beth M. Sundheim and Ralf Grishman. Message understanding conference-6: A brief history. In *Proc. of the 16th Conference on Computational Linguistics (COLING)*, vol. 1, pages 466–471, Copenhagen, Denmark, 1996. https://doi.org/10.3115/992628.992709 DOI: 10.3115/992628.992709. 42

John Sylak-Glassman, Christo Kirov, Matt Post, Roger Que, and David Yarowsky. A universal feature schema for rich morphological annotation and fine-grained cross-lingual part-of-speech tagging. In *Systems and Frameworks for Computational Morphology, 4th International Workshop, SFCM*, pages 72–93, Stuttgart, Germany, September 17–18, 2015. DOI: 10.1007/978-3-319-23980-4_5. 108

Lappoon R. Tang and Raymond J. Mooney. Using multiple clause constructors in inductive logic programming for semantic parsing. In *European Conference on Machine Learning*, pages 466–477, 2001. DOI: 10.1007/3-540-44795-4_40. 63

Damien Teney, Qi Wu, and Anton van den Hengel. Visual question answering: A tutorial. *IEEE Signal Processing Magazine*, 34(6):63–75, 2017. DOI: 10.1109/MSP.2017.2739826. 11

The National Archives. The Soundex indexing system, 2018. http://www.archives.gov/research/census/soundex.html 81

Erik F. Tjong Kim Sang and Fien De Meulder. Introduction to the CoNLL-2003 shared task: Language-independent named entity recognition. In *Proc. of the 7th Conference on Natural Language Learning at HLT-NAACL*, vol. 4, pages 142–147, Association for Computational Linguistics, 2003. DOI: 10.3115/1119176.1119195. 17

Priyansh Trivedi, Gaurav Maheshwari, Mohnish Dubey, and Jens Lehmann. LC-quad: A corpus for complex question answering over knowledge graphs. In Claudia d'Amato, Miriam Fernandez, Valentina Tamma, Freddy Lecue, Philippe Cudré-Mauroux, Juan Sequeda, Christoph Lange, and Jeff Heflin, Eds., *The Semantic Web–ISWC*, pages 210–218, Springer International Publishing, Cham, 2017. DOI: 10.1007/978-3-319-68204-4_22. 109

Dmitry Tsarkov and Ian Horrocks. Fact++ description logic reasoner: System description. In *International Joint Conference on Automated Reasoning*, pages 292–297, Springer, 2006. DOI: 10.1007/11814771_26. 34

Oriol Vinyals, Meire Fortunato, and Navdeep Jaitly. Pointer networks. In *NIPS*, 2015. 99

Xiaolan Wang, Aaron Feng, Behzad Golshan, Alon Halevy, George Mihaila, Hidekazu Oiwa, and Wang-Chiew Tan. Scalable semantic querying of text. *ArXiv Preprint ArXiv:1805.01083*, 2018. DOI: 10.14778/3213880.3213887. 24, 28

Yushi Wang, Jonathan Berant, and Percy Liang. Building a semantic parser overnight. In *ACL*, 2015. DOI: 10.3115/v1/P15-1129. 65

Warner Bros. Entertainment Inc. Her, 2013. 47

Thomas Wasow, Amy Perfors, and David Beaver. The puzzle of ambiguity. *Morphology and the Web of Grammar: Essays in Memory of Steven G. Lapointe*, 2005. 61

Gerhard Weikum, Johannes Hoffart, and Fabian M. Suchanek. Ten years of knowledge harvesting: Lessons and challenges. *IEEE Data Engineering Bulletin*, 39(3):41–50, 2016. 46

Ian H. Witten, Eibe Frank, Mark A. Hall, and Christopher J. Pal. *Data Mining: Practical Machine Learning Tools and Techniques*, Morgan Kaufmann, 2016. 40

Zhibiao Wu and Martha Palmer. Verbs semantics and lexical selection. In *ACL*, pages 133–138, 1994. 82

Xiaojun Xu, Chang Liu, and Dawn Song. Sqlnet: Generating structured queries from natural language without reinforcement learning. *ArXiv Preprint ArXiv:1711.04436*, 2017. 101, 109

Navid Yaghmazadeh, Yuepeng Wang, Isil Dillig, and Thomas Dillig. Sqlizer: Query synthesis from natural language. *PACMPL*, 1 (OOPSLA): 63:1–63:26, 2017. DOI: 10.1145/3133887. 58, 60, 64, 65, 94, 109

V. A. Yatsko, M. S. Starikov, E. V. Larchenko, and T. N. Vishnyakov. The algorithms for preliminary text processing: Decomposition, annotation, morphological analysis. *Automatic Documentation and Mathematical Linguistics*, 43(6):336–343, 2009. DOI: 10.3103/s0005105509060041. 57

Zhicheng Zheng, Fangtao Li, Minlie Huang, and Xiaoyan Zhu. Learning to link entities with knowledge base. In *Human Language Technologies: The Annual Conference of the North American Chapter of the Association for Computational Linguistics*, pages 483–491, Association for Computational Linguistics, 2010. 44

Victor Zhong, Caiming Xiong, and Richard Socher. Seq2sql: Generating structured queries from natural language using reinforcement learning. *ArXiv Preprint ArXiv:1709.00103*, 2017. 8, 65, 98, 101, 109

Jie Zhou and Wei Xu. End-to-end learning of semantic role labeling using recurrent neural networks. In *ACL*, 2015. DOI: 10.3115/v1/P15-1109. 10

Authors' Biographies

YUNYAO LI

Yunyao Li is a Senior Research Manager and Research Staff Member with IBM Research - Almaden. She is also a Master Inventor and a member of IBM Academy of Technology. Her expertise is in the interdisciplinary areas of databases, natural language processing, human-computer interaction, machine learning, and information retrieval. Her contributions in these areas have led to over 50 research publications, more than 20 patents granted or filed, multiple graduate-level courses (including 2 Massive Open Online Courses), and billions of revenue generated from technology transfer. She is widely recognized in these areas both within IBM and by the external research community, and regularly serves on prestigious program committees, editorial boards, and review panels. Her current research interest focuses on taming unstructured and semi-structured content to enable the building of new generations of AI applications for the enterprise. Yunyao is also passionate about improving the diversity for the STEM field. She has been actively mentoring women and under-represented minorities for over ten years. She received her Ph.D. and master's degrees from the University of Michigan, Ann Arbor and undergraduate degrees from Tsinghua University, Beijing, China.

DAVOOD RAFIEI

Davood Rafiei did his undergrad work at the Sharif University of Technology, his M.Sc. at the University of Waterloo, and his Ph.D. at the University of Toronto before joining the University of Alberta, where he is now Associate Professor of Computer Science and member of the Database Systems Research Group. His areas of expertise, which span over databases and the Web, is on managing large complex data. In particular, his research interest includes natural language data management and integration, spatial analysis and mining of web content, similarity-based queries and indexing, and web information retrieval. Davood regularly serves in the program committees of major database and data mining conferences (such as SIGMOD, VLDB, KDD, ICDM, CIKM) and Web conferences (such as WWW). Davood has spent time, as a visiting scientist, at Google (Mountain View), Kyoto University, and the University of Paris Descartes.

Index

Printed in the United States
by Baker & Taylor Publisher Services